ECONOMIC REFORM IN THE PRC

Also of Interest

† *China's Economic Development: Growth and Structural Change,* Chu-yuan Cheng

† *China Briefing, 1981,* edited by Robert B. Oxnam and Richard C. Bush

† *The Chinese Agricultural Economy,* edited by Randolph Barker and Radha P. Sinha

† *Food for One Billion: China's Agriculture Since 1949,* Robert C. Hsu

† *China: A Political History, 1917–1980,* Fully Revised and Updated Edition, Richard C. Thornton

† *China Among the Nations of the Pacific,* edited by Harrison Brown

† *China in World Affairs: The Foreign Policy of the PRC Since 1970,* Golam W. Choudhury

Technology, Politics, and Society in China, Rudi Volti

† *China's Four Modernizations: The New Technological Revolution,* edited by Richard Baum

Urban Development in Modern China, edited by Laurence J. C. Ma and Edward W. Hanten

Foreign Intervention and China's Economic Development, 1870–1911, Stephen C. Thomas

The Chinese Ministry of Foreign Affairs, 1968–1980: Revolutionary Politics Versus Continuity, Daniel Tretiak

China Geographer: No. 11: Agriculture, edited by Clifton W. Pannell and Christopher Salter

† *The Chinese Military System: An Organizational Study of the Chinese People's Liberation Army,* Second, Revised Edition, Harvey W. Nelsen

† *Huadong: The Story of a Chinese People's Commune,* Gordon Bennett

† *China, the Soviet Union, and the West: Strategic and Political Dimensions for the 1980s,* edited by Douglas T. Stuart and William T. Tow

Technology, Defense, and External Relations in China, 1975–1978, Harry G. Gelber

† Available in hardcover and paperback.

Westview Special Studies on China and East Asia

Economic Reform in the PRC: In Which China's Economists Make Known What Went Wrong, Why, and What Should Be Done About It
edited and translated by George C. Wang

In February 1978, the post-Mao leadership revealed an ambitious ten-year program (1976–1985) with a $600 million capital outlay, aimed at propelling China into the front ranks of the industrialized nations by the year 2000 through the modernization of agriculture, industry, science and technology, and defense. The new leadership soon realized that such a program could hardly be implemented without reforming China's economic system, which—modeled in the 1950s after that of the USSR—has been plagued by structural imbalance, inefficient management, and an overcommitment of resources to capital construction projects. By the end of 1978, a policy of "readjustment, consolidation, restructuring, and improvement of the economy" had been introduced.

In this book, distinguished Chinese economists offer candid analyses of the strengths and weaknesses of the present system. Their lucid and penetrating comments on the virtues—and drawbacks—of that system lend insight to our comprehension of China's economic problems and the country's prospects for the future. Each article is based on firsthand information and data, much of which is available here (in English) for the first time.

George C. Wang is a professor in the School of Management and the Department of Economics, California State University, Dominguez Hills. While he was a Fulbright Senior Fellow and visiting professor at Hong Kong University, he conducted seminars at the Chinese Academy of Social Sciences in Beijing. Dr. Wang is author of *Fundamentals of Political Economy* (1977) and *An Outline of the Compilation Work for an Input-Output Table for the People's Republic of China* (1956).

ECONOMIC REFORM IN THE PRC

In Which China's Economists Make Known What Went Wrong, Why, and What Should Be Done About It

---

edited and translated
by George C. Wang

Routledge
Taylor & Francis Group
LONDON AND NEW YORK

First published 1982 by Westview Press, Inc.

Published 2018 by Routledge
52 Vanderbilt Avenue, New York, NY 10017
2 Park Square, Milton Park, Abingdon, Oxon OX14 4RN

Routledge is an imprint of the Taylor & Francis Group, an informa business

Library of Congress Cataloging in Publication Data
Economic reform in the PRC.
Bibliography: p.
Includes index.
Contents: China's economy in retrospect and prospects / Xue Muqiao – The system of economic management in a socialist country / Xue Muqiao – China's modernization and the prospects for its economy / Xu Dixin – [etc.]
1. China – Economic conditions – 1949-1976 – Addresses, essays, lectures. 2. China – Economic conditions – 1976- – Addresses, essays, lectures. 3. China – Economic policy – 1949-1976 – Addresses, essays, lectures. 4. China – Economic policy – 1976- – Addresses, essays, lectures. I. Wang, George C.
HC427.9.E34 338.951 82-4914
AACR2

ISBN 13: 978-0-367-01918-1 (hbk)
ISBN 13: 978-0-367-16905-3 (pbk)

To: Jo Anne
Pearl
Andrew
Kenneth
James
Joan

Contents

Preface

For a period of more than twenty years after the founding of the People's Republic of China in 1949, China maintained little contact with the Western world. The lack of dialogue, particularly between the United States and China, precluded any normalization of their strained relations. Because of the paucity of information, studies on China in the past were more pedagogic inferences based on secondhand sources than scientific research based on firsthand data.

On February 28, 1972, former President Richard Nixon and late Premier Zhou Enlai signed the Shanghai Communiqué, thus symbolizing the end of twenty-three years of containment and confrontation and the dawning of a new era of conciliation and rapprochement. In a short span of ten years, 1972–1981, the two countries established diplomatic relations and granted reciprocal most-favored-nation tariff treatment. Since the normalization of relations, the U.S.-China trade has grown by leaps and bounds; from a few million dollars in 1972 to probably over US$6 billion in 1981.

The two governments have also exchanged numerous delegations and scholars and have concluded several agreements, especially in the fields of science and management and in matters affecting trade relations. On December 28, 1979, thirteen social scientists and humanists—representing the Joint Committee on Contemporary China (of the American Council of Learned Societies and the Social Science Research Council) and the Committee on Studies of Chinese Civilization—undertook a visit to China.

In March 1980, at the invitation of the Economic Information and Agency in Hong Kong, a Chinese economic delegation visited Hong Kong and conducted several seminars there, including one at the University of Hong Kong. Xu Dixin, vice-president of the Chinese Academy of Social Sciences, headed the delegation. Six papers were presented at the conference, covering China's economic policies in general and foreign trade and investment in particular.

In the fall of 1980, another Chinese economic delegation visited

Hong Kong, this time headed by the renowned Chinese economist Xue Muqiao, formerly vice-minister of the State Planning Commission and director of the State Statistical Bureau and now adviser to the commission. At this seminar, five papers dealing with various aspects of the economic reform were presented.

On March 23–28, 1981, the Chinese Academy of Social Sciences and the Stanford Research Institute International jointly sponsored a symposium on world economy in Hangzhou. For the first time in three decades, Americans and Chinese shared a table to exchange candid views, despite their differences in value systems and in social orders.

This book is a collection of ten papers from the above-mentioned conferences and seminars, and the papers give English readers the Chinese views of the strengths and weaknesses of China's economic system, its achievements and setbacks, its therapies and prospects. These articles are addressed not only to China specialists, but also to people who are interested in a more general overview of international trade and economic development in China.

The editor wishes to express his gratitude to the authors for their permission to have the papers translated and published in English. I am particularly indebted to Xu Dixin and Yu Guangyuan, vice-presidents of the Chinese Academy of Social Sciences; Xue Muqiao, adviser to the State Planning Commission; Chan Parkqun, editor-in-chief of the Economic Information and Agency; professors Dong Furen and Liu Guoguang; and Rio Liang for helping with the pinyin spelling. I am indebted to Megan L. Schoeck, copy editor, and Deborah J. Lynes, associate editor, of Westview Press for their painstaking work and professional advice, which saved me from many errors.

Additionally, I would like to acknowledge the generous financial and administrative support provided by the United States International Exchange of Scholars Agency, California State University, Dominguez Hills, and the University of Hong Kong. Needless to say, without the personal efforts of the individuals and the support of the institutions, this book would not have been possible.

George C. Wang

Introduction

George C. Wang

The People's Republic of China is in the throes of a sweeping reform of its entire economic system. This reform is China's fourth modern attempt to overhaul a now-faltering system, which grew out of years of protracted guerrilla war and was modeled in the 1950s on the system of the Soviet Union.

During the 1949–1952 period of rehabilitation and the First Five-Year Plan (1953–1957), China's economic performance was impressive, but after 1958, it faltered, and it has never regained the momentum of those early periods. As a result, there have been repeated calls for reforms.

The beginnings of those major reforms date back to 1958 when the revolutionary government first decided to relinquish some of its central powers of economic control. At that time, 87 percent of the Chinese state enterprises, which had been managed by various central government ministries, were turned over to local provinces, municipalities, or autonomous regions. However, that change in management merely shifted the level of administration, and the enterprises remained as appendages of various local ministries and departments. Ultimately, those enterprises that were handed down to local governments during this first reform were returned to the control of the central government, and by 1961, economic management had slipped back to its pre-1958 centralized structure.

In 1964, a second reform took place. This time, the central government delegated to local governments the power to allocate funds and construction materials for nonindustrial projects, such as communication systems and water conservation projects. This reform, too, fell short of its goal, and the system again reverted to its original, centralized rigidity.

A third reform was launched in 1970. Of a total 400,000 state-run enterprises, the managerial control of some 2,000 large ones was once again transferred to the local provinces, municipalities, or autonomous regions. In allocating resources to these key enterprises, the controlling power was shared by the central government and the various local governments.

Like the previous attempts, this reform again failed to fundamentally restructure the economy; i.e., to allow an enterprise to operate as an independent economic entity, responsible for its own profits and losses. Judging by the reports and literature now available, observers can reasonably assume that at least some of the Chinese economists and planners were aware of the drawbacks but were unable to carry out any really meaningful reform as long as Mao Zedong remained alive and in power.

By early 1977, the new post-Mao leadership had already begun to try again to rejuvenate the Chinese economy by reinstating the four modernizations program, which had been announced a few years earlier by the late Premier Zhou Enlai. Indeed, the goal of this massive program was to propel China into the front ranks of the industrialized nations of the world by the year 2000 through modernization of agriculture, industry, science and technology, and defense. To lay the groundwork for achieving the four modernizations, a ten-year economic program (1976–1985) with very ambitious targets was drafted and revealed in February 1978.

It did not take long for the new leaders to recognize that the plan simply exceeded China's resources and capabilities. By 1978, a nationwide survey of China's natural resources, capital construction requirements, and available trained manpower, as well as research into the existing economic management practices, had given Chinese planners a much firmer grip on their nation's economic problems. By the end of 1978, the central leadership had concluded that a new three-year period of economic reform (1979–1981) was necessary.

A rolling policy of "readjustment, consolidation, restructuring, and improvement of the economy" was introduced. This new policy called for a readjustment of the imbalances among various basic industries in the national economy and for a significant shift of national resources away from heavy industry and into agriculture and light industry. Further, resources were proportionally allocated to housing, education, and scientific research. In the heavy industry sector, efforts were directed toward increased output of coal, oil, electric power, transportation, and building materials—all areas in which supply is lagging behind demand. Relief of shortages in these areas alone, it has been reported, can raise China's industrial output by 30 percent.

Since the introduction of the Ten-Year Plan in 1978, production goals for key commodities, such as grain and steel, have been revised downward. A number of steps have been taken toward a retrenchment in capital construction investment, including investment for such extensive projects as the Baoshan Iron and Steel Complex and the Daqing Petrochemical plant.

These current reforms have affected not only China's domestic economy but China's foreign trade as well. The shift in priorities from heavy industry to agriculture and light industry has resulted in an increase in China's imports of grain and cotton from the United States and a scaling-down or suspension of further imports of certain capital goods from Japan.

Why did an economy that performed reasonably well during an early period of economic development run into various difficulties after 1958? What are the strengths and weaknesses of an economic system that evolved out of protracted guerrilla warfare and, after liberation, was modeled on the Soviet Union's system? Can the drawbacks and shortcomings be solved within the timetable set by the ambitious program?

Most Western studies on China and its economy have historically been based on fragmentary data and unverifiable sources, but since the normalization of relations between the United States and the People's Republic of China, there has been a sudden and active exchange of scholars and information. More recently, the reinstatement of China as a member of the World Bank and the International Monetary Fund has made available further vital statistics on that country's economic development. For the first time in more than three decades, it is now possible to make scientific economic studies of China and to draw objective conclusions.

This book is an attempt to find the answers to many of the questions directly from the work of Chinese economists and planners themselves. Each of the ten articles following addresses some aspect of the current economic reform, and each was selected for its contribution to an understanding of the problems facing the Chinese economy and the proposed antidotes to solving China's economic ills. Obviously, informed readers will not accept the Chinese economists' views presented here without applying their own reasoning and analyses. Yet to study China without listening to the Chinese economists presenting their views about their own problems would be a totally incomplete study, if not a biased one.

The initial chapter by Xue Muqiao, former vice-minister of the State Planning Commission, was chosen for its totally realistic assessment of the achievements and failures of the Chinese economy over the past three decades. Xue pinpoints where, when, and how the economic policies went astray. During the 1949–1952 period of rehabilitation, when peace and order were finally restored, China's economy grew at a rapid rate. Despite a war-devastated society, the ambitious First Five-Year Plan (1953–1957) was successfully carried out, and it laid the foundation for a more modern economic structure. Xue himself attributes this success to effective policies pursued during the period 1949–1957.

After 1958, the economy faltered. Xue blames a slowdown in agriculture on haste in collectivizing the ownership of land, farming tools, and agricultural animals. Another blunder cited by Xue was China's lopsided stress on developing heavy industry at the expense of not only agriculture and light industry but general Chinese living conditions—particularly housing, hospitals, medicine, and education.

All of those failures dampened the Chinese people's enthusiasm and hope for any realistic improvement in the nation's standard of living. Not until the post-Mao leadership came into power did the Chinese government have an opportunity to address the failed policies of the past and attempt to reform the system. Although asserting the continuing necessity of planning for economic development, Xue contends that the implementation of any plans should rely more on the proper role and use of the marketplace, and pricing and fiscal policies, than on administrative decree. He is confident that once reform is completed, the economy will regain its lost momentum. He warns clearly, however, that modernization of an ancient China cannot be achieved overnight.

Xue's second article was chosen for his penetrating analysis of the drawbacks in China's economic management system. Xue points out that in a system in which enterprises are not held responsible for their own profits and losses, they have little incentive to improve the quality of their products or to lower costs. Nor will workers strive for high productivity in a system in which they can always be hired but never fired. Xue attributes all these difficulties to an overcentralization of economic power in the hands of the state.

All economic activity in China is planned by the state, and fixed production and sales targets are handed down to various regions and enterprises with little attention paid to local and regional conditions or climate. Such a centralized and rigid system runs directly counter to any principles of division of labor.

One of Xue's great contributions in this book is his drawing of conceptual differences between microeconomics, i.e., the rational behavior of enterprises, and macroeconomics, i.e., the role of the government. In the past, Chinese decision makers seem to have confused the government's function, which is to formulate policies and lay down rules conducive to economic development, with the enterprises' own function, which is to turn out products that are high in quality and low in cost. The difference is a vital point in analyzing and understanding China's present economic reforms.

To overcome China's difficulties, Xue suggests the following reforms: (1) the enterprises should be responsible for their own profits and losses; (2) instead of the state's randomly allocating resources, local enterprises receiving construction funding or working capital ought apply to state banks for the money; (3) enterprises should retain the right to reduce the work force, when necessary, and to dismiss employees, when justified; and (4) responsibilities of managers, chief engineers, accountants, and Party committee members should be clearly defined so that one does not interfere with another.

The third chapter, by Xu Dixin on the characteristics of the Chinese approach to the problem of industrial modernization, was chosen for Xu's practical suggestions for reforming the present system. Xu, vice-president of the Chinese Academy of Social Sciences and a renowned economist who has visited the United States several times, stresses the necessity of proceeding with the four modernizations in accordance with the realities of the situation in China. Since China is over-populated, Xu contends it should adopt labor-intensive methods in this modernization, and since the economy is woefully underdeveloped, Xu calls for an acceleration of development through the importation of advanced technology and modern industrial equipment.

Xu predicts that China may have to import complete sets of plants during the 1980s. He foresees that the nation will gradually develop its own technology and learn how to manufacture its own modern equipment. He expects some sectors of the Chinese economy may even slow down during the period of readjustment, which will temporarily affect imports, but such a pause is necessary, according to Xu, for it will pave the way for future development. Once the readjustment is complete, he anticipates that the economy will grow at an even faster rate than before.

The fourth chapter, by Dong Furen, a member of the Chinese Academy of Social Sciences, deals with the problems of optimizing levels of accumulation of capital, which will maximize rates of economic growth. Dong traces China's present accumulation to three major sources: (1) the rents peasants paid to landlords before the liberation are now being tapped for capital formation; (2) the immense wealth amassed by "bureaucratic capitalism" under the Guomindang—probably also by Japan during World War II—is now being converted into productive capital; and (3) the current rapid increase in national income.

Dong focuses his analysis on the relationship between the level of accumulation and the rate of economic growth. He points out that although the national income grew at a high rate during 1949–1957, consumption and accumulation rates both rose steadily. Investment was efficient—for every 100 yuan accumulated, an output of 35 yuan was generated—and the economy reached full employment in 1956. All those accomplishments were achieved with a relatively low level of accumulation—about 24 percent of the national income—while foreign loans, mostly from the Soviet Union, accounted for less than 2 percent of the state budget.

In contrast, during the Great Leap Forward, the level of accumulation rose sharply, and the rate of economic growth plunged. This situation reminds people familiar with Keynesian economics of the "paradox of thrift." In China, however, the fall in the rate of growth was not so much due to a deficiency in aggregate demand as to shortages of capital goods and building materials brought about by a higher level of accumulation. Consequently, many existing factories operated at less than full capacity, and new projects under construction were suspended or left unfinished. The same 100 yuan, Dong demonstrates, generated far less output than before, and the rate of growth slowed down.

Although one recognizes that Dong's empirical study of China's accumulation/output ratios for the past thirty years is a contribution to the literature, it must be pointed out that in an economy in which agriculture is a predominant sector, fluctuations in the ratios can be caused by changes in the weather. Further studies are badly needed to determine how much of the slowdown in economic growth was due to overaccumulation and how much to unfavorable Chinese weather conditions.

The fifth chapter, by He Jianzhang, deputy director of the Economic Research Institute, was chosen for his systematic treatment of the errors in China's economic policies. His analysis focuses on four areas: (1) policies for rural areas; (2) policies on the collectivized economy and individual enterprises; (3) policies on competition and comparative advantages; and (4) policies on pricing.

One of the worst blunders of China's policies in the rural areas, according to He, was the blind pursuit of egalitarianism and too much haste in pushing farmers to join communes. Those ill-conceived policies dampened the peasants' enthusiasm and adversely affected agricultural production.

In cities, in the collective economy sector—such as restaurants or handicrafts—as well as in the individual economy sector—such as repair shops or house services—everything was hastily organized into state-run departments. He Jianzhang claims that this policy not only brought inconvenience to people, but also created substantial urban unemployment.

Another policy error cited in this chapter was China's one-sided stress on autarky for individual regions and enterprises. There was a great deal of overlapping between enterprises themselves and duplications within regions, but little competition anywhere. The policy weighed against the very principles of division of labor and of comparative advantage.

He Jianzhang calls for reform of the present price system. Many commodity prices are above cost, and others are below cost. The suggestions he makes are (1) the state set the rules by which the local governments can administer prices, (2) the state set the limits within which prices may float, and (3) the enterprises be allowed to adjust prices in light of seasonal fluctuations or variations in supply and demand. Although He's chapter is a contribution toward improving China's present price system, it falls short of specifying how to determine the value of the factors that go into a product. As long as costs of production cannot be scientifically determined, it will be difficult to have any price system that will lead to an optimal allocation of scarce resources.

The sixth chapter, on the restructuring of the management of China's present economic system, was a paper presented by Liao Jili at a seminar held in Hong Kong in 1980. Liao, a senior member of the State Planning Commission, finds the present structure, patterned after the economic system of the Soviet Union, incompatible with the complexities of any modern operating economy.

Liao points out four major drawbacks. First, the economy is so centralized and the enterprises so tightly controlled that neither local governments nor the enterprises themselves have an incentive to practice economy or increase efficiency. Second, all geographic regions, regardless of comparative advantages, were told by the state to produce the same or similar products. Thus, all enterprises, ignoring intrinsic interindustrial relationships, which are dictated by production technology and market forces, strove for autarky. This practice ran headlong into the principle of division of labor and became a stumbling block to any increase in technology.

Third, Liao attributes past economic chaos to inflexibility of state planning, which left few options open for regions and enterprises to exercise their own discretion. The last, but not the least, defect in the economic structure, according to Liao, was an egalitarian wage scale. (For a labor force of 400 million, wage scales consisted of only eight grades, ranging from approximately 35 to 120 yuan per month.) The contribution of this chapter lies not so much in these analyses as in its up-to-date study of the current experiments in local enterprise self-management.

Chapter 7, by Liu Guoguang and Zhao Renwei (the former an academician in the Chinese Academy of Social Sciences and the latter a senior researcher in the same academy), was selected for the insight it throws upon the role of the marketplace in China. The authors blame the failure of the marketplace to play a greater role in regulating economic activity on a misconception held by some Chinese economists who contend that economic planning and the marketplace are mutually exclusive: The more extensive the planning, the better the economy. The two authors hold the contrary view that economic planning and the marketplace are complementary and propose that in the current reform, the marketplace must be allowed to play a greater role in regulating economic activity.

They say that in the absence of the marketplace, commodity transactions will require either barter or ration and allocation. If carried out by barter, the division of labor is impeded, which will cause a return to a primitive economy. If carried out by state rationing, the enterprises may produce items that are not what people need; or conversely, what people need may not be produced. Moreover, without a marketplace, there is no way consumers can express their preferences, and it is difficult to determine what should be produced and how much.

As the two authors also point out, many commodity prices in China no longer reflect actual costs because of restrictions on the role of the marketplace. These restrictions not only breed waste in production but preclude any practice of economic accounting. Although the authors suggest allowing the marketplace to play a greater role in regulating economic activity, they do not spell out clearly how economic planning and a real marketplace should be integrated.

The eighth chapter, on foreign investments in China by Ji Chongwei (a senior member of the Commission for the Administration of Imports and Exports), was presented at a world economy symposium held in Hangzhou, China, in 1981. Ji predicts that China will continue to pursue an outward-looking policy for the present as well as for the foreseeable future. High priorities for foreign investments in China will be accorded to development of energy, particularly coal and petroleum; transportation and communications; and other small or medium-sized projects that require little investment but that can lead to quick and lucrative return.

Historical foreign investments in China, Ji says, have taken many forms, but long-term loans are now the primary source of the country's external finance. China is reported to have reached agreements with Japan, the United States, and members of the Common Market for a total loan amount of more than US$20 billion.

Up to now, however, little of these loans has been used, partly because of high interest rates and partly because the equipment and machinery imported by China in the late 1970s were more than China could absorb or utilize. As a member of the World Bank and the International Monetary Fund, however, China now has access to Special Drawing Rights and other credit lines from those two UN agencies.

Another form of foreign investment, the joint venture, means that foreign investors provide the technology and equipment and China comes up with the land, the labor, and the raw materials. Most of the joint ventures are to establish hotels, public services, and some manufacturing. China has also signed contracts with foreign companies to exploit its offshore oil. A fourth form of foreign investment is called compensation trade, i.e., China will use the finished product to pay for the foreign investment employed to produce it. Finally, China is earning foreign exchange by leasing its own land and facilities.

The ninth chapter, on China's foreign trade, by Zhang Peiji (deputy director of the International Trade Research Institute, Ministry of Foreign Trade), was chosen for its analysis of the new trends in that country's foreign trade. In contrast to the past, the central government encourages certain provinces and municipalities to engage in foreign trade and to tap their own comparative advantages. The quality of their exports is emphasized rather than their quantity. Representatives of the local producing enterprises join teams from the central ministry of Foreign Trade to negotiate the contracts.

As for China's trade prospects in the 1980s, Zhang predicts the country will continue to import grains, cotton, and industrial equipment and export textiles, nonferrous metals, and petroleum. Once the present reform efforts are completed, Zhang expects the volume of trade to grow at a much faster rate.

It is pointed out, however, that China must first work out a realistic pricing system, a rational international division of labor based on its comparative advantages, and an efficient as well as a comprehensive world trade network, including insurance, banking, shipping, and market research. Without such a well-coordinated, coherent system, it would be difficult for China to make a really significant breakthrough in its international trade.

Chapter 10, by Dong Furen, is concerned with the transformation of ownership of the means of production. This analysis was selected for its insight on the question, What led to China's historical economic blunders? Dong puts the blame on misconceptions that were embedded deeply in the minds of the Chinese high authorities who made the strategic economic decisions. They held the view, wrongly according to Dong, that public ownership of the means of production is unconditionally superior to collective ownership and that collective ownership is preferable to individual ownership.

Guided by this misconception, the Chinese leaders pushed

prematurely for collectivization and communization throughout the country. Chinese peasants were not ready for such sharp social changes, so they slaughtered their livestock and destroyed their orchards, both dampening people's enthusiasm and retarding agricultural production. In the cities, too, peddlers, repairmen, and other traditional individual and personal services were hastily turned into state-run enterprises. By 1960, Dong reports, there was not one single-individual labor enterprise operating in Beijing. Unemployment emerged, and entire trades of individual-service businesses were wiped out.

Another misconception held by the high authorities was that despite the underdeveloped state of the economy, China could skip the stage of commodity production in which products are distributed to each according to his work and enter communism, under which products are distributed to each according to his needs. Legitimate claims of compensation for work performed were seen by the high authorities as an evil legacy of capitalism that should be eliminated, and the sooner the better. And finally, Dong says, state ignorance of what the Chinese people saw as their welfare and material interests caused even further setbacks in the Chinese economy.

The ten chapters, though different in approach, share the conviction that the nation's economy will resume its thrust of sustained growth once the policy errors have been threshed out and the drawbacks removed. It is difficult to evaluate that assertion. Economic development is a highly complex process involving a host of tangible and intangible factors, and their actions and interactions, but measured in terms of the tangible factors, i.e., the advanced technology and modern industrial equipment, China's prospects for achieving its goals before the year 2000 are promising.

It is the intangible factors that the nation will have difficulty dealing with. The critical question for China, and other developing countries, is how to mold, within a short span of time, work ethics, incentive, morality, and above all, a mentality that fits modern life and is conducive to economic growth. Such an attitude can be developed, but it may take more than twenty years.

1
China's Economy in Retrospect and Prospects

Xue Muqiao

Since the founding of the People's Republic of China thirty-one years ago, our socialist economic construction has made giant strides. For example, in 1979, we turned out well over 34 million tons of steel, ranking fifth in the world; 635 million tons of crude oil, ranking ninth; 12,000 million meters of cotton cloth, ranking first; and 330 million tons of grain, ranking second. However, because of the overgrown population, these products are low when measured in per capita terms. Out labor force stands at 400 million, of which 300 million are peasants engaged in farming, animal husbandry, forestry, fishing, and other sideline occupations. The remaining 100 million work in manufacturing, transportation, commerce, services, education, cultural affairs, public hygiene, and other fields. Although the people's standard of living is still low at present, their basic necessities are ensured, and they lead a secure life, free at least from grinding poverty.

Since the founding of the new China, the population has increased nearly 80 percent (efforts are being made to bring it under control), agricultural production has risen 3.7-fold, and industry has risen a total of 42-fold (light industry 22-fold and heavy industry 98-fold). The reason that heavy industry has grown so fast is because of its low base and the backward state of development in the past.

Looking back, we feel we overstressed the development of heavy industry so there was disproportionate growth among agriculture, light industry, and heavy industry and the balance of the economy was upset. Moreover, repeated errors in policy slowed down agricultural production and the production of consumer goods that use farm pro-

Originally entitled "Zhungguo Jingji Fazhan De Huigu He Zhanwang," this paper was delivered at a seminar held at the Chinese University of Hong Kong, October 1980. Xue Muqiao was the head of the Chinese economic delegation that visited Hong Kong.

duce as inputs; therefore, since production could not keep pace with the people's ever-increasing demand, the improvement of their standard of living was impeded.

During the period of rehabilitation, 1950 through 1952, both industry and agriculture grew fast, and the standard of living was notably enhanced. From 1952 to 1979, average personal consumption rose from 70 yuan to a little over 200 yuan, or an increment of 90 percent in constant prices. As you all know, these figures were rather low compared with the world levels, but if it were not for socialism, many Chinese would have suffered from cold and hunger.

In general, our industry has grown fairly fast in the last thirty years. Aside from the spectacular rates of growth during the period of rehabilitation, industry grew between 1953 and 1979 an average of 11 percent a year, and agriculture rose at a moderate annual rate, about 3.4 percent. Apart from exogenous factors, such as an overgrown population relative to the scanty arable land, the only moderate rate of growth was attributable to our haste in transforming the ownership of the means of production. Beginning with the land reform in 1950 to the completion of the cooperativization in 1957, our performance fared reasonably well, and agriculture grew fairly fast. But we committed an error in 1958, prematurely pushing the commune movement. Although the error was rectified in 1961, leftist tendencies frequently cropped up, particularly the "ultraleftist" line pursued by the Gang of Four during the Cultural Revolution, which inflicted heavy losses on agriculture.

Although industry developed fairly rapidly during this period, we made the mistake of blindly pursuing speed at the expense of efficiency. As a result, we overextended our scarce resources in economic construction, especially in heavy industry. Between 1958 and 1960, during the so-called Great Leap Forward, heavy industry rose 2.3-fold (1960), and capital construction, 1.8-fold (compared to 1957), thereby adversely affecting agriculture and the people's standard of living. After the five-year adjustment (1961–1965), the economy recovered. Scarcely had it resumed its upward trend in 1966 when the Cultural Revolution broke out—a ten-year catastrophe during which industrial production fluctuated precariously between high and low. Because of the sabotages of Lin Biao and the Gang of Four and their ultraleftist line, work discipline slackened, management disintegrated, and the economy was pushed to the verge of bankruptcy. Had there not been those two setbacks, though different in nature (the former was an ill-conceived blunder, and the latter was a plotted conspiracy), the economy could have grown faster.

After the smash of the Gang of Four, we swiftly overcame the chaos, and industrial production resumed an upward trend in 1977 and 1978 at a rate around 14 percent a year. However, the policies of the ultraleftist line were not entirely rectified, and the recovery of agriculture in 1977 was slow. When the errors in Party line were finally corrected, agriculture grew about 8 percent a year (1978 and 1979). Economic development has proceeded fairly well, and the people's livelihood has notably improved over the last three years. Unfortunately, our gross underestimation of the protracted damage to the economy by Lin Biao–Jiang Qing's ultraleftist line, our inability to grasp the positive and negative lessons of thirty years of economic construction, and our vain attempt to recapture the lost ten years led us to another blunder. In 1978, we once again sharply raised the rate of capital construction to 36.5 percent (of national income), thus approaching the highest level reached during the three years of the Great Leap Forward. That rate, therefore, further aggravated and exposed the imbalance of the economy.

Since the economy suffered grave damage during the Cultural Revolution, what we should have done after the smash of the Gang of Four was to go through a period of rehabilitation, so as to alleviate the people's strained lives. Our failure to do so constituted another error. Fortunately, that error was promptly corrected, and a resolution was adopted at the 1979 National People's Congress to readjust the economy by scaling down the planned capital construction for that year by 20 percent. Concomitantly, procurement prices for agricultural products were raised 22 percent, which lifted the peasants' income considerably. Raised also were wage scales and bonuses. As a result, the average wage scale rose by 7 percent in 1978 and 7.6 percent in 1979 in constant prices. In the last two years, when the ultraleftist line in rural areas was halted and when the procurement prices of farm produce were raised, agricultural production grew faster than planned. The rapid expansion of agricultural production coupled with the rise in wage scales led to a brisk market and a substantial increment in supplies of urban commodities, particularly foodstuffs. Meanwhile, workers' and peasants' savings in the banks multiplied. Naturally, the Chinese people are pleased.

Another error in our work was our wavering and indecision in scaling down capital construction. By the time we finally reached a decision after long-drawn-out discussions, requisition orders for equipment for new plants had already been placed. In addition, local governments continued to add new projects, one after another. As a result, the number of actual projects being completed in 1979 was slightly greater than in 1978. In 1980, we were determined to trim down state capital construction but anticipated a rise in construction to be carried out by local governments and enterprises (the economic reform raised local government revenues and the profits retained by enterprises). Now we are determined to hold the level of capital construction for this year to the same level as last year. So, the rate of accumulation declined to 33.6 percent last year and will probably decline to 30 percent this year. For the next two to three years, we shall continue to hold down capital construction while enhancing the people's standard of living. True, accumulation, as a rule, is the primary source of expanded reproduction, but it can be counterproductive if carried too far. At the current low level of production, the accumulation rate should remain somewhere around 25 percent (of the gross national product) or at most, 30 percent. Otherwise, it will not only depress the people's livelihood, but it will also slow down production and construction and even retard economic development. Haste makes waste.

When the 1979 plan was drafted according to the readjustment policy, the rate of industrial growth was deliberately set at 8 percent. In effect, the realized rate was 8.5 percent. What is particularly thrilling is that for the first time, in contrast to the past, priority is accorded to agriculture and light industry over heavy industry. Light industry grew at 9.6 percent a year; agriculture, 8.6 percent; heavy industry, 7.7 percent. However, in 1977 and 1978, we still blindly went after speed; consequently, economic performance was not very satisfactory. To fulfill plan targets that did not pay attention to market demand, enterprises often turned out products that were low in quality and high in cost. As a result, shortage and glut existed side by side. In this case, high rates of growth will not do people any good. So, since 1979, we have reduced speed and enhanced efficiency, and the situation has begun to improve. Although the rate of growth for this year is less than the preceding two years, the overall performance is much better. Pursuing the same policy in 1980, we further reduced the rate of growth to 6 percent per year. Industrial production in the past eight months exceeded the planned rate by a wide margin, with light industry growing faster than heavy industry, which indicates that the readjustment is beginning to take effect.

Over the past thirty years, the proportions between agriculture, light industry, and heavy industry have undergone some significant changes. In 1949, agriculture accounted for 70 percent of the gross value of industry and agriculture; light industry, 22 percent; and heavy industry, 8 percent. By contrast, in 1979, agriculture declined to 29.7 percent, light industry rose to 30.7 percent, and heavy industry soared to 39.6 percent. Within heavy industry, product processing expanded so fast that supplies of energy and raw materials fell behind. Nor could transportation and communications keep pace with agriculture. Accordingly, our economic reform calls for readjusting the ratio between accumulation and consumption; i.e., lowering the level of capital construction, raising people's standard of living, speeding up the development of agriculture and light industry, and slowing down that of heavy industry.

Since any further development of agriculture rests primarily on the enthusiasm of the 300 million peasants, the commune, the production team, and the production brigade must have the power to make their own decisions. Apart from the task of raising grain production, rural communes and individual households should be encouraged to diversify economic activities, including the development of sideline occupations. Grain procurement prices should be raised whenever state revenue permits. Meanwhile, we should promote scientific farming and selectively push for mechanization.

Although light industry has a good start, its equipment is obsolete, and raw materials are scarce, which is why we must focus our attention for the next few years on innovating and renovating existing factories and on securing fuel and raw materials. To accommodate the ever-increasing demand for a higher standard of living, we must improve the quality and variety of products.

Ostensibly, modernization of the national economy calls for developing heavy industry and transportation. But at present, heavy industry is out of balance; supplies of energy and power cannot keep pace with the processing industry, and transportation is lagging behind demand. Therefore, to solve these problems, the economic construction for the years to come will concentrate on a number of projects such as extensively exploring petroleum, introducing advanced technology into the coal mines, building more thermal and hydroelectric power stations, and speeding up construction of railroads, ports, and communication facilities. These improvements will pave the way for large-scale economic development in the future.

In the past twenty years, we neglected improving people's living conditions, particularly in housing and hospitals, and science and education. To speed up the tempo of modernization, we must raise not only an army of scientists and technicians, but also a great number of economists and management personnel.

While readjusting our economic work, we have to reform the management system. In the semifeudal and semicolonial old China, the economy was so underdeveloped that production in the countryside was primitive, and production in the cities was rudimentary. Built on such a weak base, it is no wonder that the Chinese model of socialism has a low level of state ownership. Over the past years, we experienced success as well as frustration in the socialist transformation of agriculture. Whenever we were overhasty in prematurely pushing the transformation, we tended to disrupt the productive forces. Some aspects of the management system that we copied from the Soviet Union in the 1950s were appropriate for China, others were not. Our major blunders stem from the fact that we failed to understand that a socialist economy is primarily a commodity economy built on public ownership of the means of production. Instead, we denied the enterprise and the production unit their right to make economic decisions and their responsibility for profits and losses, as well as their right to trade commodities through the market. We treated the socialist economy as if it were a monolithic entity that could be run by the planning commission of the central government. The system of unified collection of revenue and unified appropriation of funds through the state budget and the system of unified procurement and distribution deprived the enterprise of its independence and initiative. Apparently, such a system was detrimental to healthy economic development.

According to Marxist theory, a socialist economy is based on socialized, large-scale production, and its prerequisite is a fully developed commodity economy. But the rural commodity economy and the urban socialized production are still underdeveloped, and our economic management system must be restructured so as to be conducive to developing a commodity economy based on large-scale production. It is necessary, therefore, to fully utilize and apply to our socialist economy that aspect of the market mechanism that has been well established in capitalist countries over the past 200 to 300 years, and thus to coordinate various economic activities through the market rather than through administrative directives. To be sure, a socialist economy must practice planning, but the implementation of a plan cannot depend on administrative arrangement alone. We must make proper use of the market, price policy, fiscal policy, and monetary policy to fulfill plans. What we stress frequently is the integration of economic planning with the market, i.e., fully utilizing the market under the guidance of the plan. That idea is a new discovery for the Marxist theory of socialist construction, and we have begun to tackle the problem in theory and in practice. Today, I cannot further expound this issue, and I will leave it to my colleagues.

Recently, economists in Hong Kong expressed their concern about the economic reform in China. They have made valuable contributions to this issue, but they are worried by China's piecemeal approach. Indeed, a national economy is an integral whole, and fragmentary reforms offer no comprehensive solution. We, too, realize that we have to fundamentally restructure the economy, but the difficulty is that the economy is in the process of readjustment. Figuratively speaking, we may compare the economy to a gravely ill person suffering from the ten-year catastrophe brought about by the Cultural Revolution, who is so fragile that he could hardly withstand "open-heart surgery." What he needs is time to recuperate. But China cannot wait too long to recover from the catastrophe. So, we begin with some minor reforms, which we hope will extend gradually to the entire system. The overriding goal of the restructuring is to decentralize state control (on both the central government and local government levels) to let the enterprise make its own decisions, to get workers involved in management, to integrate economic planning with the market, and to switch from running the economy by administrative orders to running it by economic measures and legal procedures.

These were the courses we trudged over the past years. At this juncture, we have merely some rough ideas about the future structure of the economy and must leave the specifics to be worked out through practice and experience. Obviously, even the current minor readjustments may challenge the established system. If this indeed happens, such a challenge may do the reform some good, for it may expose some of the hidden contradictions (such as the irrational prices) and thus help us chart our future course of action.

Readjustments of the economic system will result in a quickening of the tempo of development and greater efficiency. Since the readjustment drive is still in progress and the reform is yet to be completed, we have not incorporated the favorable factors in the draft of next year's plan. To avoid any repetition of past errors, the planned rate for next year's rate of industrial growth is set at 6 percent; for that of agriculture, 4 percent; and for national income, 5.5 percent. There is plenty of room for revision. Although we are certain that we can fulfill the planned targets for industry, we are not so sure whether the amount of agricultural products will exceed that of last year because of adverse meteorological conditions. Despite unpredictable adversity, the expansions in sideline occupations by communes and individual households will continually raise peasants' income. Barring unexpected disasters, the rates of growth for agriculture and industry will be higher next year, i.e., the planned targets will be fulfilled.

You all know that China is striving to modernize its socialist economy before the end of this century. In the past, some of our comrades harbored the illusion that by that time, every department and every sector of our economy would have reached the world's advanced levels of production. This is impossible, for China has a large population and an underdeveloped economy. Peasants account for 80 percent of the population, and the levels of development between sectors of the economy are exceedingly uneven. China's economy is estimated to be twenty years behind those of the advanced countries, and the situation is even worse with respect to agriculture. Within China, there are striking disparities in the levels of development that may be centuries apart. Apparently, it is not feasible that every county and every province could attain advanced levels at the same time. From the vantage point of the economy as a whole, we can only expect to achieve modest progress, i.e., to reach a level slightly above the world's average. In commenting to a foreign visitor, Vice Premier Deng Xiaoping maintained that China's goal is to reach US$1,000 (at current value) in per capita gross national product by the year 2000. Although this seems to be a modest goal, remember that per capita income now is merely US$250. Obviously, it will be no easy job to quadruple it within the given time dimension.

At the rate of growth of this year or next year, our gross national product can only double every twenty-three years. Hence, people worry whether we may be able to reach the goal of US$1,000 by the year 2000. Note, however, that this is a period of readjustment. In the future, the economy, particularly industry and agriculture, will grow faster. Besides, the reform is bound to further spur the productive forces, thus accelerating the development of agriculture and industry. During the First Five-Year Plan period, our national economy grew on the average of 8.9 percent a year, grossly exceeding the rate required (7.7 percent) to double national income every ten years. Some people noticed that in capitalist countries, where national income tends to grow in a normal year between 5 and 6 percent, China's rate is regarded as rather high. It is not likely that it can grow higher. However, it should be pointed out that although the rate of growth in capitalist countries is subject to the constraint of market demand, China's is not. If it were not for the market constraint, the rate of growth could be as high as 10 percent a year in capitalist countries. In China, we have a market of nearly a billion people, and at present, most supplies fall short of demand. When the readjustment is completed, investment will rise, and people's income will substantially increase. Even when industrial production does indeed expand 10 percent a year, it still can hardly catch up with demand. Hence, China's rate of growth can surpass that of the capitalist countries.

Some contend that even if China's per capita income should reach US$1,000, it would still be lower than that in Hong Kong and other places. One should bear in mind, however, that the Chinese population is approaching 1 billion, while fewer than 100 million people live in the industrial and commercial metropolis of Hong Kong where the per capita income stands well over US$1,000 or even US$3,000. In Shanghai, too, the per capita income has exceeded US$1,500. Besides, in estimating national income, China differs from the Western countries in concept and methodology. The national income account in China does not include services; moreover, the amount of state allowances and subsidies to workers and employees is greater than their wages and salaries. By the time the per capita income in China equals that of Hong Kong, the Chinese real standard of living will be higher than that of Hong Kong. China's problem lies in that between 70 and 80 percent of its population is peasantry, whose income is low. To raise peasants' income takes time. We hope that when the urban people become prosperous, their prosperity will gradually proliferate to the countryside.

Modernization in China must proceed from the premise that the country has an overgrown population and an underdeveloped economy but is richly endowed in natural resources. With a few exceptions such as electronics, etc., we should develop more labor-intensive and fewer capital-intensive industries. Agricultural mechanization should be carried out as soon as possible, but only in areas such as the northeast provinces; we should not blindly seek labor-saving projects in other areas. The key to the problem is how to raise production. Advanced technology may be appropriate for some industries, and moderate technology for others, but there is no way we can eliminate semimechanical or manual labor. Even in countries as advanced as the United States, manual labor still prevails in some trades such as restaurants. It would be an illusion if one fancied that all trades and all areas in China could simultaneously acquire advanced technology. When the Chinese model of modernization is achieved, the levels of science, technology, and the people's standard of living will be greatly enhanced, and the gaps between China and the advanced countries will be narrowed. We can even expect to surpass them in some fields of science and technology.

You are concerned about China's participation in international economic cooperation and its interest in seeking external funds to finance its imports of advanced technology. Over the past two or three years, we have pursued an open policy, actively seeking foreign investment. The problem, as mentioned above, lies in that we are now in the process of scaling down capital construction in order to correct the imbalances in the economy. Because of our lack of experience, we were overhasty in 1978 in seeking foreign funds and in importing advanced technology. The contracts we signed in that year extended beyond our capacity to absorb, and yet negotiations for new ones continued. At present, our energy supplies, transportation facilities, and administrative setup are all inadequate to accommodate large-scale foreign investment. Take for instance, the Baoshan Iron and Steel Complex and a few petrochemical works that are either under construction or about to break ground. They will not be able to operate at full capacity when completed due to lack of power and raw materials. Should this situation be allowed to continue, it would affect China's ability to amortize foreign debts and could adversely affect the country's credit standing in the future.

Because of the above-mentioned reasons, we have to pursue a policy of steady progress regarding imports of advanced technology and potential foreign investment. For the next three to five years, we shall undertake more projects that require less capital but offer fast turnover, and we shall refrain from projects that call for vast capital investment and slow gestation. Thus, some projects that are currently under negotiation have to be postponed. This may arouse suspicion and even disappointment among some foreign consortiums, but as far as I know, the majority of economists with broad vision maintain that the policy we are pursuing is a wise one and that the Chinese leaders are realistic.

As for the existing irrational practices and regulations in the management system, the bureaucracy and red tape that impede progress, we will surely straighten them out. In effect, that is exactly what we are doing. As you all know, China lived in seclusion for so long that it has little experience in handling international economic relations, nor do we have an adequate commercial code to govern such undertakings. That is why we are working on these problems now. It takes time to master such techniques and acquire the knowledge. One of our purposes in visiting Hong Kong is to learn from you.

The current glut in the international capital market will not be over soon. China, on the other hand, is short of capital, and it can use the funds and technology of the advanced countries. From a long-term viewpoint, cooperation between China and foreign countries has a bright future; it is beneficial to both parties. China has a territory extending over 9.6 million square kilometers endowed with rich natural resources. When the readjustment of the national economy is completed, its industrial and agricultural production will grow faster, the scale of economic construction will gradually expand, and the people's livelihood is bound to improve markedly under the new economic policy. By that time, we will be able to use more foreign capital. So, China has the potential of being not only the world's largest domestic market but also one of the largest international markets. We hope economists all over the world can visualize the bright prospects for China's economic development and join us on the basis of equality and mutual benefit. The Chinese are trustworthy people. They will never forget or treat unfairly those friends who have lent their support to China in its endeavor toward modernization.

2
The System of Economic Management in a Socialist Country

Xue Muqiao

The Present Economic Management System

After the establishment of socialist public ownership of the means of production, a socialist country must set up a system of economic management suited to such ownership. We should not assume that the socialist system will automatically demonstrate its superiority once the means of production are placed under socialist ownership. A sound system of management speeds up the development of productive forces, and an unsound one hinders it.

The benefits of the socialist economic system are mainly twofold. First, since the means of production are under public ownership, the state may utilize the nation's manpower and material and financial resources according to a plan and regulate all economic operations in the country in a unified way, avoiding a waste of manpower and, as a result, other resources. Second, since the system of exploitation has been abolished and all working people have become masters in production, the state may achieve a high rate of economic growth by making full use of the initiative and creativeness of the central government, the local governments, the enterprises, and the laborers. These two aspects of the superiority of socialism are both interrelated and contradictory. If unified state leadership over the economy is interpreted as centralized management and is allowed to weaken the power of the local authorities and enterprises to manage their own affairs, our economic life will stagnate, and the enthusiasm and initiative of the local authorities, enterprises, and working people will be dampened. Such a system of management would become an obstacle to the

This chapter is a slightly abridged version of Chapter 8 of Xue's book, *China's Socialist Economy* (Beijing: Foreign Languages Press, February 1980). The Chinese title of the chapter is "Shehuizhuyi Guojia De Jingji Guanli Tizhi."

development of productive forces. On the other hand, overemphasis on independent management by the local authorities and enterprises and a weakening of unified state leadership over the economy would lead to anarchy.

China's present system of economic management is modeled after the Soviet one adopted during the Stalin era, and it is characterized by overcentralization. The targets set by the central government are dictated to the local authorities and enterprises regardless of their suitability. The country's revenue and expenditures are all controlled by the central government. Except for specified allocations to local governments, all kinds of financial revenue are delivered to the central government. All investments in expanded reproduction and all public undertakings are handled by the central government, which allocates them to the ministries for reallocation to local authorities, enterprises, or institutions for designated uses. On the local level, a sum of money may only be used as designated, and only a small portion of the local tax income is at the disposal of the local authorities. The enterprises turn over to the state not only their profits but most of the money set aside to cover depreciation costs, which is likewise under the control of the central government. As for the distribution of products, the capital goods are allocated by state organs, and the consumer goods are purchased and marketed by state commercial agencies.

The advantage of this system lies in the state's concentrated use of its financial and material resources on projects vital to the economy. Its disadvantage lies in a neglect of the special needs of localities and enterprises, which cannot make a rational use of their own manpower, materials, and financial resources. Rigid control fetters initiative and is therefore detrimental to the achieving of a maximum of economic results through a minimum expenditure of resources.

Centralization by the central government actually means decentralized control by its different economic departments. It is impossible for the leading economic organs of the central government—including the State Planning Commission, the State Economic Commission, and the State Capital Construction Commission—to take charge of the economic operations in every industry or trade; some have to be left to the ministries. Although over a dozen ministries under the central authorities are in charge of production, they still cannot attend to all economic work. Every ministry has several bureaus, each of which is responsible for a particular trade. In addition, there are departments in charge of finance, material supplies, and the country's labor force. The flood of directives issued by the departments to the local authorities makes it impossible for them to achieve an overall balance in their regions. In making arrangements for projects to be built, ministries and bureaus often want only to make their job easy and so fail to consult with the localities and other ministries and bureaus. This practice cuts the economic ties between the industries and trades and runs counter to the principles of specialization and coordination, which must be observed in large-scale industry. Many of our factories, large and small, tend to be all-inclusive because the present system of management compels them to rely on no one but themselves. A system of administrative control that separates the inherent connections between economic operations—that is the basic defect in our economic management system.

In reforming the economic management system, we must adhere to the socialist road and pay attention to the following two principles. First, adhere to a planned economy, use correct methods of planning, and give full scope to the initiative of the local authorities and the enterprises. The state should incorporate all economic operations in the country in a unified plan and, under the guidance of this plan, directly or indirectly coordinate the activities of all departments, all areas, all enterprises, and all collective economic units. At the same time, we must understand that as China's productive forces, especially those in agriculture, are still at a low level and the socialist relations of production in the country are still imperfect, our planning should combine relative centralism with a certain measure of flexibility. Different methods of management should be adopted for the two kinds of public ownership. The economic sector under collective ownership should enjoy more independence than the sector under ownership by the whole people. There are also differences among enterprises owned by the whole people, and it is impossible to handle all of them in a single way. Planning can only provide the general direction and the key ratios of economic development, not the details. It is necessary to bring into play the initiative and vitality of the local authorities and the enterprises instead of moving them like beads on an abacus. We should let them handle everything they can, give them more power and responsibility, and combine the interests of the central government, the local governments, the enterprises, and the laborers.

Second, make sure that our economic management system gradually develops in the direction of specialization and coordination in the course of agricultural and industrial modernization. This factor is essential for large-scale, highly socialized production, and in this respect, we have much to learn from the useful experience of developed capitalist countries. For the present, we have to take into consideration the fact that China's agriculture is still a partially self-sufficient economy, but it will change in the direction of specialization and coordination sooner or later.

The degree of socialization of China's industrial production remains at the international level of the late forties, and the present system of economic management is unfavorable to specialization and coordination and to our efforts to catch up with and surpass the advanced world's level. Management along administrative lines of division—i.e., a management divided up among the central ministries or among the local governments—cuts off the links between industries or areas and does not conform to the principles of specialization and coordination. Such an administrative setup for economic management should gradually be replaced by economic organizations that transcend the barriers between industries and regions. Breaking through the dividing line between the two systems of ownership may enable state enterprises and collectives to establish joint ventures that would combine production with marketing on the basis of specialization and coordination.

In line with the above two principles, the present reform of our system of economic management should fulfill two urgent tasks. One is to change the management system in the enterprises, including the collectives, so as to give vigor and vitality to these grass-roots units. The other is to change the system of management of the national economy so as to adapt it to large-scale socialized production and thus remove the obstacles to socialist modernization. These are highly complicated tasks involving many aspects of our economic life, such as the circulation of products, the wage system, the price control system, and the planning system.

In reforming our system of economic management, we may draw on the experience of other socialist countries and some capitalist countries, but we should proceed from our actual conditions and should not mechanically imitate what is done elsewhere. At the same time, we should be aware that because the present system has remained in force for years, many people are used to it and a change in the system will affect the interests of many quarters. Thus, change is likely to be handicapped by conventional ideas and meet with resistance. We must be bold in our thinking and action. At the same time, we must be practical in our work and continually gain experience through experimentation.

Reforming the Management of State Enterprises

State enterprises are the grass-roots units of business management under ownership by the whole people. Under the guidance of state planning, the enterprises should have the power to handle their financial, material, and manpower resources and should endeavor to obtain a maximum of economic results through a minimum expenditure of resources. Under the existing system of management, however, state enterprises submit to unified state control over their income and expenditures and receive state allocations for all their spending, which is known as "everybody eating the rice cooked in one big pot." Workers are hired but not fired, promoted but not demoted—a phenomenon we call an "iron rice bowl." Many comrades mistake these practices as signs of "the advantages of socialism." In fact, they are remnants of the supply system used during the revolutionary wars and have become a major obstacle to socialist modernization.

An enterprise in a capitalist country assumes exclusive responsibility for its profits or losses and enjoys full right of management. To survive market competition, it tries its best to improve production technology and management and to reduce the consumption of manpower, material, and money. The purpose is to bring in a maximum profit by using a minimum of capital. Under the capitalist system, production is unplanned and unorganized on a national scale, which causes astonishing waste, but it is carefully calculated, planned, and organized by a particular enterprise or monopoly group. We may learn a lot from their methods of management, which are based on several hundred years of experience. A socialist enterprise must change its backward methods of management, metaphorically compared to everyone using an iron rice bowl to eat what is cooked in the same big pot. Otherwise, it will be impossible for socialism to triumph over capitalism by creating a higher degree of labor productivity.

An enterprise trying to improve its management must be granted some independence in using its human, financial, and material resources; in procuring its materials; in production; and in sales business. In the first place, it is necessary to give it a business fund and to abolish the government's monopoly control over its income and expenditure. If an enterprise turns over all its profits to the state and has no money at its own disposal, it can barely carry on simple reproduction but cannot sustain expanded reproduction, update its technology, or carry out new construction and expansion. Preservation of such a system prevents a speedy modernization of the national economy. If a business fund is to be granted as an encouragement to well-managed enterprises, we must introduce a profit retention system, that is, a system under which the enterprises can retain part of their profits for their own use.

There can be two ways of doing this: retaining part of the whole profit or part of the extra profit. The former means dividing the whole profit between the state and the enterprise according to definite proportions. The latter means giving little or nothing to an enterprise from the profit it makes within the state quota, but much to it from the profit it makes over and above the quota or from the increase in its profit over the previous year. As conditions vary from one industry or enterprise to another, so should the proportions of profit retention. After a profit retention system is initiated, an advanced enterprise will enjoy larger funds and speedier growth than a backward one. Backward enterprises, theoretically capable of making innovations or updating their technology, cannot do so for lack of funds. The state would extend short-term loans to them on the condition that the loans would be repaid from the enterprise's increased profits.

Complicated problems are involved in introducing a profit retention system, and they should be handled by economic means. The profit margins of enterprises are determined by both subjective and objective factors. Those making a higher profit because of subjective factors, such as good management, should be rewarded, and those making more profit on account of objective factors should, in principle, turn those profits over to the state. The objective factors include:

1. The price factor. The price of many products in China varies from their value, an important factor in determining profit margin. After a profit retention system is introduced, the prices of products must be readjusted to approximate value. If the profit margins on some products are too wide and yet it is impossible to lower those prices, the extra profits should be turned over to the state in the form of product taxes so that all industries and trades will get reasonable posttaxation profits under normal management.

2. Mineral resources. Some oil wells produce a few tons a day, and others produce hundreds or even thousands. On the basis of such differences, the state should either levy different taxes on resources or introduce a system whereby the mining enterprises retain varying portions of the profit they earn over and above the assigned profit norms. The system should subsidize coal mines that have suffered losses for years because of their poor resources. If they save part of the subsidies through good management, they should be entitled to retain part of the savings.

3. Labor productivity. Differences in labor productivity result from the use of different kinds of equipment. Such differences are created by unequal sums of state investment and not by unequal degrees of effort on the part of the workers. To solve this problem, the state could introduce a system whereby the enterprises pay compensation for the appropriation of fixed assets. They may pay taxes or interest on these assets at different rates to offset the differences in profit margins.

When a profit retention system is initiated, a greater part of the business fund thus established in an enterprise should be used for technical innovation and transformation and, if possible, for reconstruction and expansion. A smaller part may be used to improve the workers' collective welfare facilities and distributed to the workers and staff as bonuses. The specific proportions should be based on the conditions in each enterprise. If the fund is large, more should be used for technological development and less for collective welfare and bonuses so that the remuneration will not vary too much from one enterprise to another. When necessary, the state may set a maximum and a minimum for such remuneration so that profit retention will not create excessive financial differences among workers.

Second, it is necessary to change the system by which an enterprise uses its fixed assets and working capital. So far, the state has allocated fixed assets to enterprises for use without compensation. If an enterprise wishes to buy more equipment, it has to apply for a financial grant from the state, for it has neither the money nor the power to expand its equipment or change its technology. Even the director of a big factory employing tens of thousands of workers does not have the power or money to build a canteen or an apartment building for the workers. He has to apply for approval and for an allocation from the higher authorities. Under such a supply system, whereby the state exercises exclusive control over the income and expenditure of its enterprises and allocates the money for all their spending, an enterprise cannot conduct its own managerial work as a business accounting unit. Since it has no say over and bears no responsibility for its property, much state money is wasted. When an enterprise applies for an investment, it tries to get as much as possible, even if part of it will remain idle. But the enterprise has no money to get the equipment needed for technical innovation and transformation. Applications for investments are often turned down by the authorities or passed on to different levels for approval, which takes a long time. This system is a serious obstacle to modernization.

The way to handle the depreciation of fixed assets in China also has to be changed. Amid the speedy developments in modern science and technology, the depreciation period of equipment was shortened to anywhere from five to eight years in capitalist countries; in China, it generally remains around twenty-five years. Enterprises in capitalist countries have to renew their equipment frequently, but ours are encouraged to make do with what is available. An enterprise has to turn over to the state most of its money to cover the depreciation of its fixed assets and can keep only some money for major overhauls. Any renewal of existing equipment must be approved and financed by the higher authorities. The use of advanced technology in major overhauls is not favored but restricted. Although an enterprise should be run with industry and thrift, the present low rate of depreciation and the irrational handling of the depreciation fund must be changed.

For this purpose, it is necessary to establish a system of compensated appropriation for fixed assets. State capital investments could be placed at the disposal of the banks, which would grant them to the enterprises for use as fixed assets. A general checkup should also be made on the fixed assets already in use. On the one hand, the fixed assets belong to an enterprise, which may transfer the surplus assets to the higher authorities for compensated use by other enterprises, or it may lease or sell them to another enterprise and use the income to buy whatever fixed assets it needs. On the other hand, these fixed assets represent an enterprise's liabilities to the state, on which it should pay interest or tax at regular intervals according to state regulations. It is likely that the bulk of capital investments would still take the form of budgetary allocations. The investments would be owned by the state but handled by the banks, which would turn over the interest payments on these investments to the state. Smaller sums of capital investment may be granted as direct loans from the banks, to which the enterprises would pay principal and interest on schedule.

The system of compensated use could also be applied to working capital, which would always be distributed as bank loans. The rates of interest on such loans could be lower for regular sums, higher for additional ones, and higher still for those used to pay for overstocked goods. This practice would help eliminate both overstocking and man-made shortages of goods as well as the waste of funds. Although the astonishing stockpiles of raw and processed materials and of finished products in various enterprises are mainly caused by defects in the current supply system, they also have much to do with the uncompensated use of working capital.

After an enterprise establishes its business fund, most of the money needed to cover depreciation should also be placed at its disposal. Instead of restricting the use of the fund, the state should encourage an enterprise to carry out technical innovation and transformation with its own money or by contracting for short-term bank loans whenever necessary. However, the usefulness of such funds has to be guaranteed by a sufficient supply of capital goods, which should be provided for in the state plan and made available in every possible way. Plans for major reconstruction or expansion, especially those for new projects, should be submitted to the state authorities for approval in the interest of balancing the supply of capital goods.

Third, it is necessary to reform the personnel system. The system of management in our enterprises should guarantee the rational use of financial and material resources as well as that of manpower. To this end, the state should allow the enterprises to organize their labor forces in line with their respective needs so that everyone may contribute his best, which would break down the "iron rice bowl" system, under which one can only be hired but not fired and only promoted but not demoted. Our socialist constitution states that every citizen able to work has both the right and the obligation to work. The nation's labor force should, in principle, be taken care of by state planning. However, the job requirements in the enterprises are highly complicated, and working ability varies from one person to another. To make the best possible use of people's talents, the state should make overall arrangements, but the enterprises should be free to select their workers and staff members, and each person should also enjoy some freedom to choose his or her job. To establish a combination of the three is a difficult and yet indispensable task.

Most of the people working in our enterprises and government institutions are equal to their jobs and have a chance to make good use of their abilities, but a small number of them are either incompetent or are prevented from using their capabilities. The state should introduce a system of vocational assessment and promotion in order to transfer those who cannot fully use their abilities to suitable jobs. An enterprise should have the power to demote those who prove to be incompetent in the course of vocational assessment. It should have the power to discharge, after discussion by the trade union, a small number of workers who have long refused to do a conscientious job or who have committed serious mistakes but refuse to mend their ways despite repeated admonitions. The discharged workers may be referred back to the labor departments for new assignments or they may be allowed to find jobs by themselves.

For years, many of our enterprises and government institutions have been overstaffed and have had a slack discipline. To change the situation, it is necessary to simplify the administrative setup, strictly review the performances of all workers and staff members, promote or demote them on this basis, and reduce the numbers so as to raise efficiency to a much higher level. Workers and staff members removed from their present jobs may be transferred to suitable ones. The young ones may be given a chance to study, and the old ones who can no longer work may retire and will be given proper care. In any case, they will not become destitute and left homeless as in a capitalist society.

To bring into full play the roles of scientists, technicians, and other people with special knowledge and skill, the state should give them the right to choose their jobs under certain conditions. Some labor and personnel departments have often assumed a bureaucratic attitude and have arranged jobs for people without regard to their capabilities. Some scientific research institutes have long failed to give proper jobs to scientists and technicians but would not let them go when they were wanted by other institutions. Some scientists and technicians had nothing to do in their own institutions, but when they found suitable jobs, the personnel departments held them back. Some scientists and technicians have not been able to do much work or to advance their studies for one or two decades, so many of their best years have been wasted. A number of China's outstanding scientists and technologists are unknown in the country until their names appear in the foreign press. Such a waste of talent must not be tolerated in a socialist society. In particular, at a time when the whole nation is working hard for modernization, such a wasteful system of labor must not be allowed to continue.

Fourth, it is necessary to change the system of leadership in the enterprises. The enlargement of an enterprise's power to manage its own affairs must be followed by a change in its system of leadership, which means establishing a system of collective leadership in which each person is responsible for a particular field of work. In the early 1950s, in view of the overcentralized leadership of enterprises in the Soviet Union, Mao Zedong criticized the system of "one-man leadership," and it was replaced by a system under which the director and vice-directors of a factory assumed responsibility for different kinds of work under the leadership of the Party committee. However, in many cases, the Party committee often took everything into its own hands and so weakened the powers that should normally be held by the director, the chief engineer, and the treasurer. The administrative officers in many enterprises have failed to establish a system of personal responsibility, which has resulted in poor efficiency and serious bureaucracy. This situation is incompatible with the requirements of modernization.

From now on, the Party committee should not exercise direct control over production or business operations. Its task is to ensure the implementation of the Party's policies and guidelines and to carry out the political and ideological work that is essential for modernization. The production and business operations should be left to the factory director, the chief engineer, and the treasurer. An enterprise should institute a strict system of personal responsibility, conduct regular checkups, and remove any cadre who is incompetent or fails to fulfill his duties. For this purpose, it is necessary to strengthen democratic management in enterprises and government institutions, to establish and perfect the system of workers' congress, and to gradually introduce elections of leaders on various levels so that the workers may enjoy the right to supervise their leaders. The initiation of true democratic management is an extremely important step in the reform of the management system in an enterprise. Without democratic management, the many measures adopted for such a reform will not work or may even bring bad results.

Reforming the Management of the National Economy

The system of management in both the enterprises and the national economy needs to be changed. As changes are introduced in the managerial system of the enterprises, the same system in the different branches of the national economy must be changed accordingly. Here I shall limit myself to two major questions involved in reforming the system of management of the national economy.

To change the system of management of the national economy, it is first of all necessary to clearly define the limits of authority of the central and local governments on the principle of "unified leadership and management at different levels." In the relations between the central and local governments, the key elements that are necessary are a change in the system of financial administration and a change in the way leadership is exercised over the enterprises.

So far, most of the tax payments and profits of the enterprises have been handed over to the Ministry of Finance through the financial departments on various levels, and the budgets of the provinces, municipalities, and autonomous regions are worked out by the Ministry of Finance in consultation with those local governments. The rich areas turn over most of their revenue to the central government, the poorer areas turn over a part or none, and the poorest areas get a subsidy. But all areas, rich or poor, only keep a tiny part of their revenue, and that can barely cover administrative expenses and expenditures for minor construction projects and public undertakings. Most of the capital investments are allocated by the central government to its ministries for reallocation to the provinces, municipalities, and autonomous regions and then to the enterprises, with each grant earmarked for a specific purpose.

The same situation often applies to the funds for public undertakings. The central ministries may withdraw any fund if it is found to be duplicated, wasted, or used for an unauthorized purpose. In fact, what the local authorities do is to combine grants from the various ministries as budgetary revenue since they have little money at their disposal. Most of their extra revenue has to be turned over to the central government, which is why the financial departments of the provinces, municipalities, and autonomous regions do not take much interest in their revenues or expenditures, and make no serious effort to increase the former or to cut down the latter. Neither do they have the power to make readjustments even if they find duplications or waste in expenditure.

A change in financial administration was tried out in Jiangsu Province a few years ago, with a division of local revenue between the central and local governments. It was agreed that the province would share its revenue with the central authorities according to a definite ratio over a period of three years, and during that period, it would be responsible for the balance of its own budget. The experiment resulted in an immediate rise in local revenue. In 1976, the national revenue dropped, but Jiangsu registered a rise. The next year, when the national revenue went up, Jiangsu achieved a big increase over the previous year.

What has been done in Jiangsu is only one of the several possibilities for changing financial management. When conditions are ripe, it will also be advisable to divide the different kinds of revenue and expenditure among the authorities on the different levels. This way, the administration of revenue and expenditure will be clearly defined for the central government and for the governments of the provinces, municipalities, and autonomous regions. Certain tax incomes will go to the central government, others will be collected by the local governments, and each enterprise will turn over its profits to the authorities in charge of its affairs. Whoever earns more may spend more, and governments on all levels will be in charge of balancing their own budgets. This practice will give greater financial power to the local authorities.

After financial power is divided between the central and local authorities, all major construction projects will still have to be built with investments from the central government, although the local governments may build auxiliary projects to render service to the major ones. Local financial resources should be used first for agricultural development and then for tapping the potential of the existing local industries through technical innovation and transformation. The local resources could also be spent on the construction of some new factories and transport facilities as well as schools, hospitals, and shops, workers' housing, and other collective welfare facilities. As things now stand, the local governments do not have enough money at their disposal to develop or expand their potential; they have accomplished little municipal construction and are unable to ease the people's difficulties. Actually, projects built by local governments make possible a fuller use of local resources and are better suited to local needs. In general, medium-sized and small projects should be built by local authorities with guidance from the higher levels. Such projects could also be handled by specialized or joint corporations as soon as they are set up.

Of course, a division of financial power between the central and local governments will not solve all problems. For example, the financial and material resources acquired by Jiangsu Province through the above-mentioned experiment are still quite limited, and the province can cater only to its own needs. Thus, it will probably cut its aid to other parts of the country. The province has a well-developed machine-building industry, which can supply many products to other provinces. But more investment and resources will be needed for Jiangsu to satisfy the needs of those other provinces; failure to acquire them will limit the cooperation between Jiangsu and the others. The southern parts of Jiangsu Province, including Suzhou, Wuxi, and Changzhou, have always had close economic links with Shanghai, with local factories, including commune factories, working on orders from big plants there. After planning is placed mainly on a regional basis, such traditional ties of cooperation will probably be weakened, which will hinder the coordination between these areas and Shanghai on the basis of specialization. Such a situation would obviously be detrimental to socialist modernization.

Moreover, since industrial development is extremely uneven among China's provinces, municipalities, and autonomous regions, the industrially backward ones urgently need support from the advanced ones for economic construction. Thus, there are contradictions not only between the central ministries and the localities but also among the localities themselves. In general, the industrially developed areas wish to acquire greater independence, and the underdeveloped ones prefer unified management and unified allocation of products by the central government. The same kind of contradiction also exists between producing and buying areas of major products such as rolled steel, timber, cement, and coal; the producers demand more power for the local authorities, and the buyers prefer unified allocation by the central government. For these reasons, it has been very difficult for the state organs of economic management to reach an agreement on changing the current system of planning and management.

What is the real trouble? It lies mainly in the contradiction between the system of administrative control and the objective requirements of economic development. The main feature of the old system of economic management in China is management by administrative setups, administrative gradations, and administrative regions. Such an artificial division of economic management along administrative lines does not conform to the objective laws of economic movement and is therefore unfavorable to the division of labor and coordination among different industries and enterprises. The development of large-scale socialized production would mean a more elaborate division of labor in production, and to meet the needs arising from the division of labor, the central and provincial governments have set up more and more ministries and bureaus. As none of the economic operations of the enterprises can be conducted in an isolated way, each has to be authorized by the many departments concerned, which often creates several months of paperwork, and sometimes a problem remains unsolved after several years. To avoid all these troubles, enterprises often stick to their old ways and act mechanically on orders from above.

Although some enterprises have been placed under the local authorities, many problems still have to be referred to the higher authorities. During the periods of the First and Third Five-Year Plans, almost all the large industrial enterprises were placed under the unified administration of the central ministries, which dampened the intiative of the local authorities in managing the economy. Some of the new enterprises built by the ministries were often wasteful duplications of existing ones, but the local authorities were powerless to do anything about this situation. In 1970, many big enterprises administered directly by the central ministries were placed under local government, but the supply of materials to these enterprises, their production, and the marketing of their products were still controlled by the ministries. With one more "boss," these enterprises only found things more difficult. Some came up against even greater difficulties because they were put under a municipal government within a province and therefore had to obey three bosses—the central ministry, the province, and the municipality. Many factories had originally supplied their products to the whole country. Some were put under a local administration, and their production was adapted to local needs, which resulted in a shortage of their former products. Originally, a few factories had produced certain types of goods for the whole country. After decentralization, each province had to build factories to produce such goods, creating much waste. Some areas, counties in particular, set up factories merely for their own interests without considering the supplies for raw materials and fuels.

The controversy over whether the economy should be managed along the vertical lines of division between the central ministries or along the horizontal lines of division between localities will not lead to a fundamental solution of the problem. Reform must center on expanding the power of the enterprises and of specialized or joint corporations, which will take over economic management from administrative organs. This reform will completely change the current system of economic management in China.

To meet the requirements of large-scale socialized production and the resultant specialization and coordination, many enterprises in capitalist countries have merged with one another to form specialized or joint corporations, which extend their operations beyond the limits of their respective industries, regions, or nations. Although our country has a different economic system, we are confronted with the same objective requirements arising from large-scale socialized production. We also find it necessary to organize various specialized corporations, such as motor vehicle corporations, and to combine many medium-sized and small plants for streamlined production. We may also set up joint corporations on a still larger scale. For example, an iron and steel corporation may simultaneously conduct mining, coking, iron-smelting, steel-making and steel-rolling operations and may also operate chemical and building-material plants through a multipurpose utilization of its resources. The equipment it needs may be made in its own plants, by other heavy machinery plants, or imported if necessary. Corporations like this should set up agencies for the procurement of raw and processed materials and fuels, sales departments, and research and design institutes.

All these establishments are placed under unified management but each should conduct its own business accounting. A joint corporation has the right to decide on its economic operations through periodic consultations with the establishments under its management without having to apply for authorization from the higher administrative organs. Some ministries have set up specialized or joint corporations without cutting down the power of their specialized bureaus. The result is an overlapping of establishments plus lower efficiency.

Specialization and coordination should be introduced not only within industry, but also between industry, agriculture, and commerce. For example, the Yee Tsung Tobacco Company, a cigarette manufacturer established by British capital in old China, built several tobacco-growing bases to get the quality raw materials it needed. We may do the same thing. Textile mills, especially those producing silk, wool or linen, should concern themselves with the production and purchase of silkworm cocoons or wool or bast fiber and then try out streamlined production based on specialization and coordination. Factories producing export commodities may also form joint corporations with both raw material suppliers and exporters. The present lines of division between raw material producers, manufacturers, and sellers do not help to improve the quality of products or increase their variety to meet market needs but merely raise the cost of production. A change should be effected step by step.

There has always been a strict division between China's industry and commerce. As commercial agencies have to both purchase and try to sell everything produced, production often does not suit demand. The central government has recently authorized commercial agencies to purchase goods on a selective basis, but this practice has created new contradictions as some agencies refuse to purchase many products in demand but forbid the producers to sell them by themselves. This situation has forced down light industrial production in many areas. Selective purchases by commercial agencies should go hand in hand with the marketing of goods by their producers. Some factories and industries set up their own marketing agencies to sell goods that the commercial agencies do not want to purchase. The marketing agencies set up by factories may also handle the repairs of certain types of goods for consumers. New products should generally be sold by the producers so that they may research market needs and improve quality.

In foreign trade, we should perhaps change the practice of trade companies handling all transactions with businessmen from abroad, with whom the producers have no direct contact. The producers should take part in trade talks and in the conclusion of contracts. They should share the foreign exchange earnings with the trade companies as well as the responsibility for fulfilling the contracts. Some producers should be authorized to establish direct cooperation with foreign businessmen and undertake jobs like the processing of imported materials. Industries and specialized corporations producing large quantities of export commodities should be permitted to set up their own import and export companies, which would operate under the guidance of the import and export business provided by various institutions.

In connection with the reform of the system of economic management, Chinese economists are discussing whether the economy should be managed through planning or through the market or whether it should be managed by administrative or by economic methods. The differences between the one and the other may be illustrated by some examples.

Capital investments may be handled in three ways. First, the government grants budgetary allocations and pays for all spending on a noncompensatory basis. This is a purely administrative method. Second, the government grants budgetary allocations through banks, to which the recipients return whatever they do not spend. This is a combination of administrative and economic methods. Third, all investments are loaned by the banks, to which the recipients pay principal and interest. This is a purely economic method. So far, we have been using the first method, but we may use the second method for investments in major projects and the third for those in small projects and technical innovations.

The circulation of products may also be handled in three ways. First, capital goods are allocated according to plan, and consumer goods are procured and marketed by state commerce. This is the administrative method. Second, the capital goods controlled by the State Planning Commission and by the central ministries are supplied by state quotas and are purchased by users from the specialized corporations according to those quotas, and the other capital goods are open to free purchase. As for consumer goods, the major items are procured by state commerce and rationed to consumers, and the other items are open to free purchase. Third, the quotas of capital goods and the rations of consumer goods are both abolished, and everything is open to free purchase. At present, we can only adopt the second method because we cannot entirely abolish the quotas and rations but can only narrow their scope. The third method can be considered only when there is an abundant supply of capital and consumer goods and when we will be able to make full use of the role of the market and balance supply and demand through our price and credit tax policies.

Production may be planned directly or indirectly. In other words, the plans may either be binding instructions or mere references. In China, direct planning has generally been applied to the economic sector under ownership by the whole people and indirect planning to the sector under collective ownership. In actual practice, the latter has often become direct planning as well. From now on, no compulsory crop targets should be set for the collectives, and much of the direct planning in the economic sector under ownership by the whole people may gradually be changed to indirect planning, whereby state plans will be fulfilled through consultations with producers and the implementation of various economic policies.

Will the organs of economic administration be abolished after the replacement of administrative orders by economic means? No, they cannot be abolished. These organs should be simplified and reduced in staff size since they will no longer handle actual economic operations, but they will still be charged with heavy responsibilities of leadership. After a fundamental change in the method of leadership, they must learn to make good use of the regulatory role of the market and greatly improve their art of leadership. The change means not a lighter but a much heavier responsibility.

The planning commissions on all levels will still work out long-term and annual economic plans to achieve overall balance in the national economy. A change from direct to indirect planning does not mean that the plans are optional. They must be carried out, but the difference lies in the means of carrying them out. In other words, the state will see to their fulfillment through consultation and by economic measures, utilizing the role of the market and the law of value and other economic laws. Compared with direct planning, indirect planning is a more complicated and difficult job, which requires a higher theoretical level and more professional knowledge on the part of the economic administrators.

The economic and capital construction commissions and the organs in charge of production on all levels will undertake to coordinate the economic operations of all industries and trades, corporations and enterprises, including those engaged in capital construction. They will help them dovetail the relations between procurement, production, and marketing; guide their development along the lines of state plans; and ensure the realization of those plans by working out economic policies and measures with the financial, banking, and price control authorities.

The financial authorities and banks will be responsible for the circulation of capital and money throughout the country. They will be empowered to examine and supervise the economic operations of the enterprises, particularly their finances, for a rational distribution of capital funds among the different regions. The labor and supply departments will study the least wasteful use of manpower and materials.

In short, the various organs of economic administration should act according to objective economic laws and develop more ways to achieve good economic management. In face of the new circumstances of the modernization drive and the tasks involved, they will have to study new problems and adopt new measures and will always have more than enough to do. Thus, it is completely wrong to assume that a laissez-faire attitude may be adopted toward the country's economic operations.

Economic Readjustment and Managerial Reform

To lay a firm basis for socialist modernization, we must first of all readjust the proportions between the different departments of the national economy and straighten out the economic order. We must also reform the system of economic management and operate the economy according to objective economic laws to lay a solid foundation for the four modernizations. Readjustment and reform must go hand in hand. Without readjustment, we shall not be able to undertake reform with a free hand, and certain reforms that are necessary and possible for the present will facilitate readjustment. But there is also a contradiction between the two. For the purpose of readjustment, it is necessary to strengthen, at least for the time being, the central authorities' unified administration of the economy, whereas reform calls for a decentralization of power. To solve this contradiction, one generally undertakes readjustment first and reform next and conducts reform during the course of readjustment and vice versa.

Many press articles discussing the system of economic management almost unanimously demand decentralization. However, most of the documents issued by the central authorities in the last couple of years lay emphasis on a unified administration of finances, banking, supplies, the labor force, wages, the prices of products, etc., pointing out the need to observe state discipline in financial and economic affairs. All of this difference of opinion reflects the different requirements arising from readjustment and reform, which seem contradictory to each other but share the same goal.

The reform of economic management places a certain measure of responsibility on the enterprises for their profits and losses on the principle of material interests. But as a result of the imbalances in the national economy, many enterprises are suffering from a shortage of raw materials, fuels, and power supply and have to suspend production from time to time. They should not be held responsible for a failure to fulfill production targets or even deficits caused by these external factors. Without solving the problems of raw materials, fuels, and power supply, it will be very difficult to appraise the performance of the enterprises and give them material incentives on the basis of their production achievements and profit earnings. Insufficient power supply compels some plants to suspend production for more than 100 days a year and prevents some newly installed plants from starting operation. A mere shift of power to the grass roots without a solution of such problems will bring the enterprises many more difficulties that they will not be able to overcome by themselves.

There is much confusion in our pricing. In many cases, prices depart from values. Products urgently needed by the state are too cheap, and those not in urgent need are too expensive. Raw and processed materials are too cheap, and manufactured goods are too expensive. Under these circumstances, if all enterprises assume responsibility for their profits or losses, the production of urgently needed raw and processed materials and of fuel will drop, or even cease altogether, and manufacturing industries will grow fast, worsening the present imbalances. The present profit margins of some enterprises are not determined by management but by prices. Without a readjustment of prices, it will be difficult to work out a rational profit retention system.

Under the present tax system, some of the tax rates do not favor a readjustment of the business orientation of industries and enterprises. More taxes are being levied on products that are vital to the national economy and the people's livelihood but are in short supply and should be produced in larger quantities, and fewer are imposed on products that should and can be limited. This system does not make for economic management in light of objective economic laws. Enterprises in many industries, especially in the mining industries, bring in different profits because of different natural conditions. For example, there are large differences between the resources and, consequently, between the profits of the Daqing Oilfield and the Yumen Oilfield. Thus different tax rates, including those on resources, should be introduced to make the profit retention system effective.

Since some enterprises get more investments and better equipment from the state, they have achieved a higher labor productivity. If the uncompensated use of fixed assets continues, the profit retention system cannot be used on a fair and equitable basis. If we are going to initiate a compensated use of fixed assets, we have to conduct a nationwide appraisal of the fixed assets of state enterprises in the first place. This is an enormous job, and it cannot be accomplished in a short time.

In summary, a reform in the managerial system requires a good job of readjustment and has to be linked with reforms in other fields. This necessity calls for overall planning and orderly progression. It is impractical to oversimplify the reform and assume that it can be carried out on the strength of a state decree.

Reform in the distribution of supplies must also be based on readjustment. Raw and processed materials, fuels, and electric power are in such poor supply that without unified distribution by the state, it will be impossible to meet the needs of vital industries and enterprises. There will be even more waste, and enterprises will have to send out more purchasing agents to hunt for supplies.

As for consumer goods, grain, cotton cloth, cooking oil, and nonstaple foods are all in short supply, and it is still impossible to abolish the state purchase and ration systems. They can only be changed step by step as production rises. For the time being, we can only change parts of the system for the distribution of consumer goods by increasing the number of circulation channels and cutting down the intermediate links. After the rural communes and their subdivisions complete their sales to the state, they should be allowed to market their surplus products on their own. This practice will speedily increase the production of foodstuffs and create conditions for a narrowing of the scope of state purchases and rations and the ultimate abolition of those systems.

The readjustment of prices is also a highly complicated task. The purchasing prices of farm produce—grain in particular—are too low and should be raised gradually. But if the selling prices of farm produce and consumer goods made from agricultural raw materials are raised simultaneously with the purchasing price of farm produce, the livelihood of the workers, particularly of those in the lower income brackets, will be affected. It is irrational to raise only the purchasing prices and not the selling prices of grain and nonstaple foods because if the former exceed the latter, the commercial departments will face deficits for a long time, and they will hardly be able to handle their business by economic means. Thus, the prices of consumer goods have to be readjusted along with wage increases.

Reform in the managerial system must be premised on a readjustment of the national economy, that is, the reform should proceed along with the readjustment. This fact does not mean that there is no way to undertake the reform under the present circumstances. While readjusting the proportions of the national economy, we may gradually carry out some necessary and possible reforms. Some of these reforms may be started right away or at an early date. Some of the comrades in the departments in charge of production are used to the existing state of affairs. They seem to have a rigid way of thinking and are full of misgivings about the reform. Our economic administrators should look at things from the standpoint of the overall situation and take a positive approach to the reform of the managerial system in the interests of modernization. On the other hand, our theoreticians should not oversimplify the reform. The national economy is a highly complicated organism, and a single change may affect the whole picture. To avoid confusion in the course of the reform, we should keep the whole situation in mind and take its possible consequences into account. Many of the reform measures should first be tried out in some regions, cities, or enterprises and then applied more widely on the basis of the initial experience. This procedure will help us avoid detours.

The purpose of both readjustment and reform is to speed up modernization. While considering the two tasks, we must also proceed with economic construction, especially the strengthening of such weak links as the fuel, electric power, and building-material industries, communications, and transport. Some sophisticated equipment will have to be imported to improve our technology. In the next few years, therefore, the state must concentrate its capital investments on key items and ask the various departments and regions to delay or suspend projects that are not urgent. We should carefully consider the economic returns of our investments, build a minimum of new projects, and tap the potentials of existing enterprises through technical innovation and transformation. The state should ensure the supply of raw and processed materials, fuels, and electric power first to enterprises that produce quality goods that are needed by the state and the people by using a minimum of these resources. Enterprises producing low-quality goods at a high rate of consumption should be instructed to suspend production and put themselves in better shape. Only after the proper readjustments are made can reform of our system of economic management proceed smoothly.

3
China's Modernization and the Prospects for Its Economy

Xu Dixin

At the invitation of the Economic Information Agency, I have come to Hong Kong to talk about the prospects for China's economy in the 1980s. I will focus on four areas of China's modernization: first, its pursuit of the program on the basis of the actual conditions; second, the characteristics of the Chinese style of modernization; third, the importing of advanced technology; and fourth, the prospects for the economy in the 1980s.

Proceeding from Actual Conditions

Historical materialism holds that the economy is the base of the social system, so the foundation of any nation, whether socialist or capitalist, inevitably rests on the economy. Since the founding of the republic and the completion of transferring the ownership of the means of production to the state, the modernization of agriculture, industry, national defense, and science and technology has become the historic task of the Chinese people. The late Premier Zhou Enlai, on behalf of Chairman Mao Zedong, clearly and emphatically brought up the great task at the Third and then the Fourth National People's Congress in 1964 and 1975, respectively. However, it was not until after the downfall of the Gang of Four that it was possible to fulfill the task.

The four modernizations program presented by Chairman Hua Guofeng to the Eleventh National Congress of the Chinese Communist Party stipulates that by the turn of the century, China's industry, agriculture, national defense, and science and technology will

This paper, entitled "Zhungguoshi De Xiandai Jianshe Ji Qi 80 Niandai De Zhanwang," was presented at a seminar on China's economy in the 1980s held in Hong Kong, March 7–8, 1980. Xu was the head of the Chinese economic delegation that visited Hong Kong.

catch up to advanced world levels. Here, I will discuss briefly the present economic situation in China and how we propose to go about modernizing in the Chinese style.

The idea of Chinese-style modernization means to modernize the country in light of the actual conditions of the economy. In the past thirty years since the liberation, China has made considerable achievements. Its efforts to modernize, however, have been frustrated by numerous difficulties. Primarily, the difficulties were and still are overpopulation and underdevelopment. Already over 450 million in 1949, the population had exploded to 960 million by 1978, not counting Taiwan. Overpopulation is a hindrance not only to improving the people's material and cultural life but also to capital accumulation and socialist construction.

Moreover, as the modernization of agriculture, industry, and technology proceeds, it is bound to raise the ratio of capital to labor, particularly manual and unskilled labor. The further modernization progresses, the more acute the problem will become. Thus, Chinese-style modernization calls for demographic planning.

At the same time, China must be realistic in managing the existing 350,000 large and medium-sized enterprises. Although China's aim is modernization, it cannot simply abandon those enterprises and start all over again. Some will be remodeled to meet the advanced world's standard; others will be renovated and brought up to date. Much attention will be paid to developing the country's traditional handicrafts and to service trades that are indispensable to industrial and agricultural production and the people's livelihood. In other words, modernization in the Chinese style means that the country must seriously take into account its 900 million people.

Prior to the liberation in 1949, China was a semifeudal, semicolonial country in which industry, agriculture, and science and technology were all in a backward state; that is, China's economic foundation was weak, and its technology, backward. Although seventeen years of efforts brought impressive results after the liberation, the gap in the levels of development in science and technology between China and the industrially advanced countries widened because of the disruptions caused by Lin Biao and the Gang of Four.

Experience demonstrates that training scientists and technicians, as well as building a solid economic foundation, requires protracted efforts. Any ill-conceived, radical, or irrational policy not based on objective reality would be detrimental to China's development, and it could take several years to correct the adverse effects. Thus, China must carry out modernization at a steady pace according to present economic and scientific levels. Steady advance does not mean no advance, it simply means to create slowly now the conditions for rapid advance in the future.

China's modernization should proceed on the basis of the fact that the country is overpopulated and its economy is backward. But China is a big country, with 9.6 million square kilometers, and endowed with abundant mineral deposits, water resources, a fair climate, and fertile land, which are favorable to developing agriculture, forestry, animal husbandry, fishery, and farm sidelines. It therefore possesses the material conditions for building up a fairly comprehensive national economic system. It will consistently make efforts to tap, explore, and fully utilize the favorable conditions in accordance with physical and economics laws.

Chinese-style modernization means the simultaneous development of industry, agriculture, national defense, and science and technology. The era of mechanization, from the viewpoint of the world's industrially advanced countries, started with the invention of the steam engine and came to an end with the Second World War. During that period, internal combustion engines, electricity, and machinery replaced manual labor. Since then, the development of electronics and computers has ushered in an era of automation. Although one of China's primary goals of modernization is to bring the means of production up to date, the demographic problem and the underdevelopment of the economy mean that the strategy of development should be mechanization rather than automation. To pave the way for further advancement, automation may be carried out only in selected areas of scientific research.

Modernization of industry, agriculture, national defense, and science and technology will inevitably lead to an increase in the gross national product and thereby gradually raise per capita income. Some people prefer to use the gross national product as a yardstick to measure a country's level of economic development. For instance, those countries with a per capita gross national product of US$3,000 are classified as middle income, and those with more than US$3,000 to US$4,000, as high-income or advanced countries.

Using the gross national product as a yardstick to measure a country's level of industrialization has its advantages; namely, it is straightforward and clearly defined. Nevertheless, used by itself—independent of the economy as a whole—it has some limitations. For example, an oil-rich country may have a per capita gross national product of US$16,000, which is higher than that of the United States, and yet it may lack a comprehensive, well-developed modern economy.

Chinese-style modernization cannot rely exclusively on a mono-product, however well developed it may be. The Chinese style means an overall, balanced development of industry, agriculture, national defense, and science and technology. It means modernization not only of the means of production but also of the structure of industry and agriculture; it means not only to streamline the relationship between agriculture and industry, which is defined as "taking agriculture as the foundation and industry as the leading factor," but also to modernize science and technology as instruments to carry out the other three modernizations.

Experience has demonstrated that without competent technicians and capable managers and administrators who can master techniques and operate advanced equipment, the modern facilities cannot be fully utilized, even when available. I think the pursuit of modernization in the Chinese style should be scientific. Obviously, as I have just said, modernization of agriculture, industry, national defense, and science and technology is bound to result in a rise in the gross national product and per capita income. Therefore, the four modernizations program is the cause, and the increase in gross national product is the effect. Can the two be integrated?

The Essence of the Chinese Style of Modernization

Chinese-style modernization is based on the socialist public ownership of the means of production. At the present stage, there are two types of socialist public ownership in China: ownership by the whole people, as manifested in the state enterprises, and collective ownership by the working people. Modernization in China can be realized only on the basis of these two types of ownership. The present economic system, which was established in the 1950s, is a highly centralized one in which economic activities are directed by state administrative organs and the enterprises have very little freedom of action. Since this system hinders development of social productivity, the state is experimenting in major cities with reforms that give enterprises more decision-making freedom in production, management, personnel, and distribution of profits.

It must be pointed out that reforming the economic system does not mean negating the socialist public ownership of the means of production. When the reform of the enterprise is completed, or in other words, when it assumes responsibility for its own profits and losses, there will be no change in the ownership. Ostensibly, China cannot construe the practice of an enterprise's being responsible for its own profits and losses as private ownership. In collective enterprises, where the level of public ownership is low, further reducing the level to a point where business activities were carried out on an individual basis would be retrogressing toward capitalism, which must be opposed.

Since the modernization drive is to proceed on the basis of socialist public ownership of the means of production, it cannot work without the proletarian dictatorship of the state, the leadership of the Chinese Communist Party, and the guidance of Marxism-Leninism and Mao Zedong thought. Some friends abroad equate China's modernization with Westernization. This view is debatable. Although in the modernization drive, China has adopted some advanced technology from the capitalist countries, learned from the Western industrialized countries, and drawn lessons from their acquired knowledge in science and management and in economic efficiency, China will never let anything impede the socialist system, the public ownership of the means of production, the proletarian dictatorship, and the principles of Marxism-Leninism and Mao Zedong thought. It is improper to equate modernization with Westernization.

One of the problems facing the Chinese style of modernization is how to reconcile economic planning with the market. The facts are that China is a socialist country with public ownership of the means of production and it has a planned economy. An extremely crucial question is, To what extent should economic activities be placed under state planning? Past experiences indicate that commodities vital to the national economy and to the people's livelihood must be placed under state planning and numerous other commodities, for which state planning is either impractical or unnecessary, should be left for the market to work out.

Socialist production and circulation could be impeded and the quality and variety of commodities could be adversely affected if state planning were overextended without paying due attention to economic realities. Shortly after the successful transformation of the ownership of the means of production in China, Comrade Chen Yun said: "The bulk of the nation's industrial and agricultural production is carried out according to state plans. At the same time, some products are turned out in conformity with the market conditions but within limits permitted by the state plan. Planned industrial and agricultural production is the mainstay, whereas free production according to supply and demand is a supplement." Comrade Chen Yun continued, "The state market is the mainstay, while the free market under state control plays a limited role."

Chinese-style modernization is bound to raise the question of how to reconcile economic planning with the market. The positive and negative experiences of the past thirty years have taught us that in building a modern socialist economy, we cannot divorce ourselves from the actual economic conditions and overextend state planning to cover too many economic activities. Nor should we forget that planned production is the mainstay of the economy and that its function is to regulate economic activities. When the current readjustment is completed, the proper relationship between state planning and the market will be established.

Import of Technology

Chinese-style modernization is based on the principle of self-reliance. That, however, does not mean isolating the country from the world or ignoring the advanced levels of science and technology and the efficiency of management achieved by other countries. The ignorant, naive means the Gang of Four employed in handling science and technology and foreign trade did great harm to the country and the people. Experience has shown that advanced technology can be imported without impairing the principle of self-reliance. On the contrary, it can enhance the country's productive capacity and boost its economy. China's position of self-reliance will be strengthened if it can adequately adapt the imported technology, modify and improve it, and gradually build its own system of technology.

Quite a few countries forged ahead under different international circumstances by importing advanced technology and then adapting it to domestic needs. Japan, for instance, took such a course and achieved spectacular results. Had the Japanese isolated themselves from the world and tried to develop their own technology from scratch, they would have taken many more years to reach the level prevailing today, and the effort would have cost them much more in research and experimentation than it actually did. From the viewpoint of saving time and money spent on research and pilot production, a planned importation of technology conforms to economic principles.

One way to import advanced technology is to purchase complete sets of plants. Usually, this is what a country would do in the early stage of modernization. However, if it keeps on doing this too long, it would waste a great deal of precious foreign exchange in imports. Habitual imports of equipment will impede the domestic machinery industry. In that case, the country would rely more and more on foreign technology instead of on domestic skills. It would forfeit the goal of self-reliance. So, by importing complete plants at the beginning, China will gradually reach the point when it will only import technology. Moreover, while importing technology, China must also tap the potentials of the existing mines, factories, and other enterprises; make the best of the production facilities available; and raise its own production efficiency. China must pay attention to such factors as the overall balance of the economy, the ability to repay international loans in foreign exchange, the capacity to engage in capital construction, as well as to the gestation of imported technology and facilities. Otherwise, the state, local administrations, and enterprises would all face a politically and economically difficult position.

In addition to importing advanced technology, China must learn how to manage modern enterprises so as to raise efficiency, that is, to obtain maximum results with minimum costs. This is not just a temporary, expedient measure. China must continue to do so even after the completion of the modernization.

Prospects for China's Economy in the 1980s

Having covered the Chinese style of modernization and the problem of importing technology, I will try to outline the prospects for China's economy in the 1980s.

The three-year period beginning from 1979 is designated for readjustment, restructuring, consolidation, and improvement. This is the first drive for modernization since the whole economy reoriented toward that goal. Because the readjustment did not actually start until the latter half of 1979, it will probably continue until 1982. Hence, modernization in the 1980s is divided into two periods: 1980–1982 and 1983–1990. First, let me talk about the three-year period of readjustment and its impact on the economy.

First of all, China will strive to achieve an all-around increase of production in agriculture, forestry, animal husbandry, sideline occupations, and fishery; to raise substantially the production of industrial and consumer goods; to improve efficiency in industry and transportation by economizing in fuel consumption and raw materials; to scale down capital construction to a level corresponding to the financial and material resources available; to trim the number of projects and streamline management; to step up exports and tap overseas funds and technology. As production expands, the incomes of peasants in the collectives and of urban workers will rise, and more jobs will be available for urban young people. At the same time, China will strengthen the weak links in science, technology, education, public hygiene, environmental protection, and urban renewal.

In general, the readjustment stresses the maintenance of balance between accumulation and consumption, between industry and agriculture, between production and construction. It calls for tapping the potentials of existing enterprises while building new ones. Since 1979, the readjustments of the proportions between the various sectors of the economy have brought about preliminary results. For instance, by raising the prices of farm products and by earnestly implementing the policy of "high pay for high productivity," the peasants' enthusiasm in most rural areas has been aroused, thus properly adjusting the relationship between accumulation and consumption. Similarly, an increase in employment and a 40 percent raise in pay for the urban workers have substantially improved the balance between accumulation and consumption in the cities. So, the relative share of consumption has risen, and that of accumulation has declined. Further adjustment this year will probably lift the ratio of consumption to 70 percent of national income, and that of accumulation will decline to 30 percent. Clearly, to maintain the proper relationship between accumulation and consumption is one of the important factors of economic development, for a rational readjustment of the balance between the two will directly or indirectly affect the relationships between production and consumption, between industry and agriculture, between light industry and heavy industry, and between output and capital construction.

Although readjustment is the key to the economy, it is closely interrelated with three other factors, namely, restructuring, consolidation, and improvement. Restructuring refers to the overcentralization of the economic structure. By and large, the present restructuring of the economy consists of giving local administrations more power in handling their financial affairs, in giving enterprises more freedom in making decisions, and in reorganizing industries into various corporations according to the division of labor. Today, there are some 350,000 industrial enterprises in China. The central government can hardly run all of them efficiently, such as mobilizing the initiative of the local authorities and arousing the enterprises' enthusiasm. Those that consistently operate at loss or turn out inferior goods that are not in demand should be consolidated, and those that are beyond salvage should either temporarily suspend production, convert to other lines, or simply shut down. When the economy has completed readjustment, restructuring, consolidation, and improvement, it will enhance the technology, management, and production of all industries and enterprises, and thus, a solid foundation will be laid for further progress in socialist construction in the next seven years.

At the end of the readjustment, the economy will look like this: First, grain will no longer be accorded a predominant role in agricultural production. By then, planted grain acreage will account for 80 percent of the country's cultivated land, and other economic crops will constitute the remaining 20 percent. Reduction in grain acreage does not mean less grain production. On the contrary, per unit grain yield will rise because of expanded irrigation and drainage systems, of the ever-increasing availability of chemical fertilizers and insecticides, and of mechanization and electrification.

By 1990, it is forecast that the grain output will be over 400 million tons per year. As attention will be paid to the development of forestry, animal husbandry, sideline occupations, and fishery, their share of production relative to that of grain will rise. The ratio of the output value of forestry, animal husbandry, sideline products, and fishery to grain (including economic crops) was 32.3 percent to 67.7 percent in 1978. This lopsided agricultural structure, which could and probably did have adverse ecological effects, has been corrected under the current readjustment. In the 1980s, the economy will achieve a better ecological balance, whereby agriculture will be developed more comprehensively than it is now, and whereby production will be more rationally arranged than it is now.

Second, China will discard the blind pursuit of iron and steel production. It is true that iron and steel are indispensable to socialist modernization, but China cannot afford to turn out iron, steel, and their products that do not meet the specifications with regard to quality and variety and then let them lie idly in warehouses.

During the three years of readjustment, therefore, there will be an improvement in the quality and variety of iron and steel rather than an increase in quantity. It is on that basis that iron and steel output is expected to rise steadily in the later 1980s. By 1990, steel production will probably be double the present level. In the next few years, the existing oilfields and coal mines are to be reorganized, and energy production will not rise much. But when more funds are available for investment in the late 1980s than in the early years, productive capacity and production will expand at a faster rate. It is not improbable that coal production will rise by 100 million to 200 million tons above the present level and that the output of crude oil will rise by tens of million tons, or even double the present level. In the process of readjustment, China has begun to correct the lopsided stress on developing heavy industry at the expense of light industry. This correction will ensure a rapid development of textiles and light industry in the later years of the 1980s. Likewise, no effort will be spared to increase variety and improve quality.

Third, restructuring the economy will eliminate the current bureaucratic mode of management whereby enterprises are not responsible for profits and losses. Everyone, so to speak, "eats out of the same big rice pot." After the readjustment, when one cannot "eat out of the same big rice pot," an enterprise will be responsible for its own profits and losses, and it will have to try its best to market the product. Thus, enterprises are bound to compete with each other, not only in production but in circulation as well. Which enterprise will get ahead? Ostensibly, the one whose products are in great demand, low in cost, and superior in quality will win. As the restructuring of the economy proceeds, competition between enterprises in production and circulation will inevitably grow keener and keener. In fact, such competition has already begun during the period of readjustment and will certainly become more lively in the later years of the 1980s. Competition under socialism is not analogous to competition under capitalism. Under socialism, it is a lever that constantly spurs socialist enterprises to increase production and to improve management and yet creates no antagonism because socialist enterprises are either state owned or collectively owned.

Fourth, two years ago, China started importing advanced technology, and the number of contracts signed in 1978 alone exceeded the total of the past thirty years. Bearing in mind the principle of self-reliance, China nevertheless will increase imports. During each of the last seven years of the 1980s, the volume of imports will be greater than that for 1978. Imports of technology are subject to some restrictions, which include the country's capacity to absorb and gestate new technology and new equipment and the availability of foreign exchange. To build up its foreign exchange reserves, China must step up exports and expand the tourist industry, in which there is great potential. Therefore, both exports and the tourist industry are expected to rise above the present levels in the later years of 1980s.

While China's socialist construction forges ahead in the 1980s, so will China's relations with industrialized countries. A strong and prosperous socialist China serves the interests of peace-loving people the world over and is a reliable force for all countries that oppose hegemony and aggression. There is no doubt that China's drive for socialist modernization will draw attention and support from peace-loving countries and their peoples.

It will not be an easy matter to bring China's agriculture, industry, national defense, and science and technology close to the advanced world's level by the end of this century. In striding forward, China will face all kinds of difficulties, but its goal will be achieved. China has the correct Party line and is a stable and united nation; it has a competent and hard-working labor force, administrative personnel, and scientists and technicians in various branches of production; and it has the support and concern of friendly countries. All of China's difficulties will certainly be overcome.

4
The Relationship Between Accumulation and Consumption in China's Economic Development

Dong Furen

In economic development, developing countries in general face the common problem of determining the proper ratio between accumulation and consumption. That is, how does a country balance the demand for a vast accumulation of capital to purchase advanced technology and equipment against the demand for huge expenditures to raise the standard of living? China, in the course of its economic development, has encountered some of these difficulties. Sometimes, it has managed the ratio properly and achieved good results; other times, it has managed poorly and created problems. The following are some aspects of the problem:

I

Where does accumulation come from? Just as the ways to solve the problem vary, varied, also, are the means to deal with the relationship between accumulation and consumption. Some of the capitalist countries solved this problem by relying primarily on extracting the surplus from the peasants and by exploiting the colonies. China, as a socialist country, obviously cannot follow such a path.

Many a contemporary developing country relies on foreign capital. China, however, prefers not to take this course; there is the potential danger that an overreliance on foreign capital may make China a vassal of other countries. China relies on its own resources and seeks external

At the invitation of the editor, Dong wrote this article in October 1981 specifically for this book. Its Chinese title is "Zhungguo Jingji Fazhanzhung Jilei He Xiaofei De Guanxi Wenti."

funds only as a supplement; i.e., it may borrow foreign capital but does not count solely on it.

In the 1950s, when the economic conditions were extremely difficult, China accumulated capital mainly from internal sources. One of these sources was through a redistribution of wealth. The victory of the people's revolution brought an end to imperialism, feudalism, and bureaucratic capitalism as well as an end to oppression and exploitation. The plundered wealth was expropriated by the people and used, in part, for national construction; the rest was used to improve the standard of living.

Statistics reveal that the wealth pillaged by the four big families alone—Chiang, Soony, Kung, and Chen—amounted to 500 million ounces of gold, and what those families could not take with them when they fled was confiscated by the people. The land reform relieved the peasants from the heavy burden of paying a total of 70 billion catties of grain to the former landlords, who had wasted it in sumptuous consumption. After the land reform, this immense amount of wealth was saved and returned to the peasants, who used a portion of it for consumption and the rest for accumulation. As for the wealth amassed by the national bourgeoisie, it, too, was appropriated for socialist construction, except for a portion that was paid out as fixed dividends for individual shares of enterprises operated jointly by the state and individuals.

The second source of accumulation came from expanded production. The establishment of socialist production relations greatly released the productive forces and spectacularly expanded production, thus creating a source of accumulation. Since the land reform had freed the peasants from their feudal shackles and had given them whatever the land yielded, they were not only capable but eager to make investments. Their incentives soared unprecedentedly, and agricultural production repeatedly set historic records. From 1949 through 1952, the gross value of agricultural output rose, on the average, 14.1 percent a year; from 1953 through 1957, 4.5 percent a year. The rapid growth provided funds not only for agriculture but also for the national economy as a whole, including industry and other related sectors. Compounded by a reduction in the costs of production, accumulation grew by leaps and bounds. Industrial production increased 34.8 percent annually during the years from 1949 through 1952, and 18 percent for the period 1953 to 1957. Compared to 1952, industrial production costs dropped 29 percent during 1953–1957, or 6.5 percent a year.

The third source of accumulation was the practice of economy and frugality, as well as the complete elimination of waste. Whatever was saved was used for construction, and all accumulated funds were rationally allocated for investment. Diligence and frugality were cultivated, and waste and conspicuous consumption were stamped out. Simultaneously, the simplification of the overgrown state administration and the retrenchment of expenditures for national defense sharply reduced the state budget. Patriotic bonds also played an important role in capital construction during the early period after the liberation. Because of the availability of funds and the rational allocation of investment, capital was productive during this period.

The pursuance of the policy of self-reliance, however, did not preclude foreign loans. In the early years after the liberation, China received some modest loans from the Soviet Union. During the decade 1949–1959, foreign loans accounted for only 2 percent of the state revenue, and even that came to an end after the rift in Sino-Soviet relations. With the strained international situation as it was at that time, there was no way that China could get loans from Western countries. Not until the 1970s did China break the policies of containment and embargo, and consider the possibility of securing loans from developed countries. Although external financing is undoubtedly conducive to China's economic development, experience has proved that China should rely mainly on its own efforts to accumulate capital. That is what it will do in the future.

For a period of time, however, China viewed the use of foreign capital as something evil and disgraceful. That was certainly a mistake. The current economic situation in China is fundamentally different from that in the early period after liberation. Now China has built a relatively comprehensive national economy. When borrowing abroad, China should weigh carefully whether or not it is financially capable of repaying the loans and whether or not it can absorb the imported technology. A limited import of external capital will not subject China's economy to foreign control, and foreign investment is especially needed since the standard of living is still low and the economy is facing many difficulties. A controlled borrowing abroad can narrow the gap between consumption and accumulation.

Where will China obtain the material and technology for capital accumulation? Some developing countries, instead of developing their own manufacturing industry, export natural resources (such as petroleum) or primary products to obtain the necessary foreign exchange to import manufactured goods. Different countries adopt different measures to solve the problem of consumption and accumulation.

China has its own policy. Although it, too, exports some natural resources and primary products in order to trade for construction material, that is not the long-range goal. China is aware of the facts that irrecoverable resources will run out sooner or later and that it cannot build an independent national economy by permanently relying on a foreign supply of equipment and technology. There is a Chinese saying, "Modernization cannot be purchased." Being a big socialist country, China must set up an independent and comprehensive economy of its own and rely primarily on its own ability to come up with the material and advanced technology needed for economic construction.

Financially, China relied on its own sources to accumulate capital in the early period after liberation, but technologically, it imported modern equipment and material for economic construction. Prior to liberation, the state of China's industry was extremely backward. There were some light industries, consisting mostly of textiles, but heavy industry was insignificant. The steel output for 1949 was less than 1,580,000 tons, not quite 0.0001 of the world's total steel production; coal, 324,300,000 tons; electric generating capacity, less than 19 million kilowatts; and the power generated, 43 billion watts. The meager machinery industry could barely handle processing, assembling, and maintenance, and the machine-tool industry was unable to turn out even simple tools such as lathes, axles, and precision instruments. It was under these conditions that China was compelled to import advanced technology, equipment, and other materiel needed for capital construction.

During the first decade after the founding of the republic, the Soviet Union and some Eastern European countries assisted China in designing, equipping, and building 400 industrial projects and provided scientific data as well as the technological know-how for over 6,000 items. Undoubtedly, this assistance played an important role in the early period of capital construction.

At that time, China had the choice of two alternatives. One was to accord first priority to developing heavy industry and thus lay a foundation of basic industries so that China could produce its own means of production to support agriculture and light industry. The second alternative was to develop light industry first and to export those products in return for machinery, equipment, and other means of production. China chose the first course and built some modern plants for heavy industry. Since then, China has been able to substitute a portion of the imported equipment and tools with domestic products. During the First Five-Year Plan, 60 to 80 percent of the machinery and equipment was manufactured in China itself. Meanwhile, the composition of China's exports underwent some change as manufacturing and minerals rose to 28.4 percent in 1957, compared to 17.9 percent in

1952. The country not only had achieved self-sufficiency in manufacturing some machinery and equipment, but also was exporting a few products that it had formerly imported.

So, step by step, China has emerged from being a state that relied primarily on imports of capital goods to one of relative self-sufficiency. In retrospect, China seems to have chosen the right course of development. It was this self-sufficiency that enabled it to continue to get machinery and equipment needed for capital construction after the Sino-Soviet rift and under the Western blockade. China did not succumb to foreign pressure. It must be pointed out, however, that because China blindly sought complete autarky, it failed to explore the possible gains that could have been achieved through an international division of labor.

II

There is little doubt that China's exaggerated self-sufficient policy on capital accumulation created some difficulties concerning consumption versus accumulation, but experience has demonstrated that when handled properly, these difficulties can be overcome. Hypothetically, accumulation should have been harder to deal with in the early period of economic development when the economy was underdeveloped and the national productivity was low, when the people were still impoverished, and when 4 million were unemployed. Under such conditions, huge amounts of funds were required to feed the people and to gradually relieve them from poverty. All these problems called for a fast-growing economy and gigantic capital accumulation. And yet, it was during this period that China scored a great success. Not only did the country accumulate huge amounts of capital, but it also raised the standard of living at a fast rate.

During the 1950–1952 period of rehabilitation and reconstruction, China's national income rose 53 percent; the accumulated funds, 93 percent; and the consumption funds, 34 percent, or 23 percent per capita, averaging 4.3 percent a year. During the same period, the peasants' income climbed 30 percent, and wages rose 70 percent. During the First Five-Year Plan, the average national wage scale soared 42.8 percent, and the peasants' income climbed 30 percent. The level of rural consumption in 1957 had risen 80 percent compared to 1949, or 30 percent compared to 1952. By 1956, unemployment had been basically eradicated.

How did China achieve its goals? Primarily, through the three sources mentioned above. When national income is held constant, one cannot raise accumulation without reducing consumption. The people's long-range interest demanded a moderate increase in the level of consumption, which made room for a higher rate of accumulation that will raise the standard of living in the future. China did impose some restrictions on the level of consumption, but only on landlords and the bourgeoisie in order to narrow the striking disparity in consumption between the rich and the poor. This policy led to an improvement in the livelihood of the peasants and the workers, particularly those who had lived on the edge of starvation.

It goes without saying that consumption and accumulation must maintain a proper balance. Accumulation stems primarily from a rapid increase in production and a reduction in costs. It was the swift rise in the national product during this early period that made it feasible to raise both consumption and accumulation. Even assuming a constant national income, it is still viable to raise the levels of consumption and accumulation simultaneously, provided that capital is more efficiently utilized. Prior to the First Five-Year Plan, when large-scale construction had just begun and other engineering projects were still under construction, the investment/output ratio, as shown in the table, was high enough to yield a 35-yuan national product for every 100-yuan investment.

Regrettably, this healthy economic development was disrupted by policy errors. After 1958, China persistently pushed for ever-increasingly higher rates of accumulation at the expense of the people's consumption. As a result, the rate of accumulation rose from 24.9 percent in 1957 to 33.9 percent in 1958, and soared to 43.8 percent in 1959. Such high rates of accumulation resulted in grave consequences for the national economy, as they strained supplies and upset the balance between economic sectors. The ambitious construction projects consumed so much material and means of production that supplies ran short of demand. Many factories could not operate at full capacity, and some projects were either suspended or not completed. As a result, the investment/output ratio declined during the Second Five-Year Plan, and every 100-yuan gross investment yielded, as is indicated in the table, barely 1 yuan of national income.

Ironically, the high rate of accumulation failed to bring about a high rate of growth. On the contrary, the national income declined on an average of 3.1 percent a year in 1957 constant prices. The sharp rise in accumulation adversely affected the people's consumption, which slid downward in comparison with 1957. The average annual levels of consumption for peasants and workers were 79 yuan and 205 yuan, respectively, in 1957, compared to 65 yuan and 68 yuan for 1959 and 1960, and the workers' level of consumption dropped to 195 yuan in 1958.

Clearly, it was not feasible to maintain such high rates of accumulation, so, the economy retreated.

One of the series of economic reforms that ensued was a reduction in the rate of accumulation to 10.4 percent in 1962. It is regrettable that China did not learn a lesson from its past failure. No sooner had the economy turned around in 1966, than the rate of accumulation was once again hiked to 30.6 percent. Throughout the 1970s, even when the economy was gravely depressed, the rate of accumulation was well over 30 percent—as high as 36.5 percent in 1978. Although the economic conditions had improved after 1976, in comparison with the 1960s, the fact remains that too high a rate of accumulation tends to affect the national economy adversely. So, once again, China was forced to scale down its rate of accumulation. The crux of the problem is how to maintain a proper balance between consumption and accumulation. It is no exaggeration to say that the imbalance between consumption and accumulation has been the primary cause of economic setbacks in China since 1958.

One can draw many valuable lessons from a review of China's economic development. First, in pursuing a policy of self-reliance, China should exercise caution in dealing with the problem of accumulation and consumption. In order to rely on a country's own efforts to accumulate capital, it is necessary to raise both the amount and the rate of saving for a certain period of time. This procedure should be carried out only when the national income is rising and when an improvement in the people's consumption is assured. Moreover, there should be a ceiling on the rate of accumulation, for an increase in accumulation is bound to affect the people's current consumption. There are at least two approaches to this problem, and each will lead to different results. One is to gradually raise the standard of living. When the people perceive a brighter future with a higher standard of living, they will work for accumulation. The alternative is to raise accumulation by lowering the people's standard of living. This policy will diminish the people's incentive and could even lead to social disorders. Therefore, accumulation should be raised only when the people's consumption has been improved.

Second, during the course of large-scale capital construction, the level and rate of accumulation should be raised gradually within limits. Once the rate reaches a plateau, it should stay there because any sharp fluctuations in the accumulation rate would adversely affect the economy. Since the bulk of the capital accumulated is for construction projects that usually last more than a year, fluctuations in capital funds could lead to a suspension or holding up of engineering

TABLE 1
Indexes of China's Economic Growth: 1950-1979

Year	Annual Growth Rate Gross Value Agricultural Products	Annual Growth Rate Gross Value Industrial Products	Annual Growth Rate National Income	Accumulation as a Percentage of National Income*
Reconstruction & Rehabilitation Period: 1950-1952	14.1	34.8	19.3	
Heavy Ind.		48.8		
Light Ind.		29.0		
1st 5-Year Plan Period: 1953-1957	4.5	18.0	8.9	24.2
Heavy		25.4		
Light		12.9		
2nd 5-Year Plan Period: 1958-1962	-4.3	3.8	-3.1	30.8
Heavy		6.6		
Light		1.1		
Readjustment Period: 1963-1965	11.1	17.9	14.5	22.7
Heavy		14.9		
Light		21.2		
3rd 5-Year Plan Period: 1966-1970	3.9	11.7	8.4	26.3
Heavy		14.7		
Light		8.4		
4th 5-Year Plan Period: 1971-1975	4.0	9.1	5.6	33.0
Heavy		10.2		
Light		7.7		
1976	2.5	1.3	-2.3	31.1
Heavy		0.5		
Light		2.4		
1977	1.7	14.3	8.3	32.3
Heavy		14.3		
Light		14.3		
1978	9.0	13.5	12.3	3.5
Heavy		15.6		
Light		10.8		
1979	8.6	8.5	6.9	33.6
Heavy		7.7		
Light		9.6		

*Unadjusted prices
**Estimates of unadjusted prices

Accumulation as a Ratio to Increase in National Income Per 100 Yuan*	Accumulation for Material Production Purpose	Accumulation for Non-material Production Purpose**	Distribution* Total Investment	
			Material Production	Non-material Production
35	59.8	40.2	71.7	9.1
1	87.1	12.9	86.8	4.1
57	65.5	34.5	83.0	6.9
26	74.5	25.5	89.4	4.0
16	77.5	22.5	86.6	5.7
-9	82.9	17.1	85.1	6.1
27	75.2	24.8	83.3	6.9
33	75.5	24.5	82.8	7.8
32	65.5	34.5	73.0	14.8

projects already under construction, which would inflict heavy damage on not only the industry in question, but also the related industries. It is easy to conceive that had China raised the rate of accumulation gradually and modestly after 1958, rather than abruptly, it would have accumulated more capital, its economy would have grown faster, and its standard of living would have been higher than it is today.

Third, China's stress on accumulation without paying equal attention to investment efficiency was another major factor that caused its economic setbacks. After the First Five-Year Plan, the ratio of accumulation to annual national income growth declined (see table). Up to the Fourth Five-Year Plan (1971–1975), the ratio fell to less than half of that during the First Five-Year Plan. Had China paid attention to investment efficiency, it would have achieved a higher rate of economic growth and a higher standard of living.

III

No doubt, the course that China chose to develop first—heavy industry so as to obtain materiel and technology needed for capital construction—created some difficulties in balancing consumption against accumulation, especially during the early period. The policy brought about three difficulties. First, in order to rely primarily on its own efforts to accumulate capital, China needed to export large amounts of agricultural products and processed goods to pay for the imports of technology and capital goods. During the early period of construction, China imported modern equipment and technology from the Soviet Union and the Eastern European countries. With the exception of a fraction of the imports, which were financed by credit, the bulk was paid for by exports. Agricultural sidelines and processed foodstuffs accounted for 80 percent of the exports, and the rest consisted of manufactured goods and minerals. The massive exports of farm products and processed foodstuffs were only possible at the expense of domestic consumption, so the standard of living was lowered.

Second, heavy industry, being capital intensive, requires huge amounts of funds and materials. Unlike light industry, which has only a short gestation period, heavy industry usually takes many years to build. Hence, building heavy industry requires large amounts of capital and high rates of accumulation. Because of these needs, particularly in the early stage of development, heavy industry competes with agriculture and light industry for capital and materials.

Third, heavy industry relies on agriculture and light industry to provide the raw materials for its production and consumer goods for its workers. Thus, the development of heavy industry will affect the availability of agricultural and light industrial products for many years, not only in the domestic market, but also in the export market. This factor, in turn, restrains the country's capability to import materiel and technology for capital construction. These are some of the difficulties concerning the problem of consumption versus accumulation.

Past experience seems to indicate that as long as appropriate relationships are maintained among heavy industry, agriculture, and light industry—particularly after the foundation of heavy industry has been laid—the difficulties concerning accumulation are not insurmountable. Not only can certain capital goods be substituted for imports, but they can also be exported in lieu of agricultural and light industrial products. This possibility increases the available materials for agriculture and light industry for domestic consumption as well as for export.

During the first eight years of China's economic development after the founding of the republic, heavy industry grew at a relatively fast rate because it maintained proper ratios with agriculture and light industry. During the First Five-Year Plan, agriculture grew at an annual rate of 4.5 percent and light industry at 12.9 percent, higher than the 2.2 percent demographic rate of growth. Thus, even though heavy industry grew as much as 25.4 percent a year, the standard of living was still rising steadily. It must be pointed out, however, that signs of imbalances between economic sectors began to crop up at this juncture. The lack of raw materials forced light industry to operate below its capacity, and less and less, heavy industrial projects were built to support other industries. Facing these problems and drawing on the Soviet experience, China at this point pursued a corrective policy of parallel development of heavy industry, on the one hand, and agriculture and light industry, on the other, with the emphasis being placed on the former. Unfortunately, the policy was not faithfully implemented.

During the Second Five-Year Plan, the country's obsession with a high rate of growth further widened the gap between heavy industry, on the one hand, and agriculture and light industry, on the other. They were seriously out of proportion. In 1958, heavy industry grew at a rate of 78.8 percent; light industry, 33.7 percent; and agriculture, 2.4 percent. In 1959, heavy industry grew 48.1 percent; light industry, 22 percent; and agriculture declined 13.9 percent. By contrast, in 1960, light industry dropped 9.8 percent, agriculture decreased 12.6 percent, and heavy industry continued to climb 25.9 percent. As a result, the standard of living fell sharply.

After several years of adjustment, as the balances between heavy industry and light industry and between heavy industry and agriculture were restored, the faulty policy of overemphasizing heavy industry was once again reinstated during the Third Five-Year Plan. That erroneous policy brought about a decade of catastrophe. Just as before, heavy industry, light industry, and agriculture were gravely out of proportion.

Looking back over the twisted course it has trudged since the founding of the republic, China has learned some lessons on how to maintain the proper relationships among agriculture, light industry, and heavy industry. First, agriculture plays a dominant role in the national economy and is closely related to consumption and accumulation. In the first place, agriculture is a major source of capital accumulation. Apart from providing funds for its own development, it has to support industrial development. As one of the major sources of saving, agriculture channels all accumulated capital to the state through taxation and the price mechanism. The agricultural tax, however, is insignificant, accounting for 11.1 percent of state revenue during the First Five-Year Plan and 5.4 percent from 1952 through 1978. Since the historically formed price disparity between agricultural and industrial products cannot be corrected overnight, the difference between the state procurement prices and the market prices is the capital accumulated. Besides, imports of capital goods for economic construction, too, are paid for by exports of agricultural and light industrial products.

In the second place, agricultural and light industrial products are the major components of consumer goods. Over 80 percent of the raw materials used as input for light industry comes from agriculture. Therefore, the standard of living is intimately related to agricultural development.

Not only does agriculture have a great impact on consumption and accumulation, but the proper relationship between consumption and accumulation also depends on agriculture. During the early stage of the construction of heavy industry, China took a cautious approach to agricultural problems. For example, to stimulate production, the agricultural tax was stabilized at a certain rate independent of any increase in production. The terms of trade between agriculture and industry had improved so much by this time that both the peasants' income and farm production soared. In addition, the state extended credit to support agricultural development. This was an effective policy that enabled agriculture to increase rapidly. Not only did agriculture accumulate more capital, but more products became available for export in exchange for materials and technology as well as for home consumption. An adequate development of agriculture, therefore, is the key to resolving the relationship between consumption and accumulation successfully.

Conversely, most of the mistakes China has committed could be attributed to its failures concerning agriculture. For instance, an overestimation of the 1958 harvest led to an excessive state procurement of food grains. This policy, analogous to slaughtering the goose that lays the golden eggs or to draining the pond for fish, not only impeded agriculture but also undermined the relationship between consumption and accumulation.

Last year, China decided to stabilize the state grain procurement for future years at the 1971–1975 level. Moreover, as of 1980, the state will reduce levies on rural production brigades while raising the procurement prices of some staples. All of these actions will certainly play an important role in stimulating agricultural production and redress the grave imbalance between consumption and accumulation. However, any unfavorable meteorological conditions may alter this balance. Caution must be exercised when fixing ratios between consumption and accumulation so that they will not be too low in bumper years and too high in lean years, which could cause sharp fluctuations.

Second, the substitution of capital construction materials and technology imported by domestic production should be realized gradually. Nor should the construction and development of heavy industry be carried out in haste. If heavy industry developed too rapidly, and if capital were accumulated beyond what the economy could bear, consumption would be lowered. Moreover, if heavy industry were developed so fast that it became out of step with agriculture and light industry, not only would capital accumulation and the standard of living be impeded, but exports would be reduced, which, in turn, would affect imports of material and technology. Too much haste in developing heavy industry, therefore, was the major factor that repeatedly upset the equilibrium between consumption and accumulation.

To be sure, a well-developed heavy industry could potentially provide materials and technology that agriculture and light industry need, could turn out domestic products to substitute for imports, and could even export some capital goods to relieve the pressure on agriculture and light industry. Certainly, heavy industry could increase supplies of consumer goods and improve the relationship between consumption and accumulation, but there is no guarantee that these things would necessarily happen if heavy industry is granted priority. Only when all the related industries grow proportionally can heavy industry promote economic growth.

Although it is necessary to substitute domestic products for imports, the process of substitution should proceed gradually. Not everything must be produced in China. Past experience seems to suggest that whenever heavy industry is pushed too fast to substitute for imports, the result is just the opposite, for when heavy industry grows too fast, supplies of raw material fall behind, which results in a rise, rather than a fall, in imports. Correspondingly, more agricultural and light industrial products must be exported to make up for the increased imports. Often, in China, the faster heavy industry grew disproportionately, the greater was the shortage in some steel products. More of those products, then, had to be imported at the expense of consumer goods. So, a haste to substitute domestic products for imports can lead to an increase in imports.

It was an overanxiety about substitution that led China to overlook the importance of developing light industry. High profit and quick turnovers are the features of light industry. In building an economy, a proper development of light industry can raise the rate of capital accumulation, stimulate exports, increase consumption, and improve the relationship between consumption and accumulation. Therefore, to maintain a proper balance, China should not overdevelop its heavy industry in order to substitute domestic products for imports but should develop light industry to increase consumption and to raise exports.

Third, in developing heavy industry, attention should be paid to its internal structure. The industry should be structured in such a way that it can turn out products not just for itself but also for agriculture and light industry. Only then can the three sectors grow coordinately. Otherwise, shortages of agricultural or light industrial products could directly or indirectly impede the relationship between consumption and accumulation. China's long obsession with the development of heavy industry distorted its production structure. Take steel, for example: On the one hand, huge quantities of steel rods were stockpiled in warehouses, and on the other hand, there was an acute shortage of certain types of steel to manufacture farm tools, build facilities, and produce chemical fertilizers, insecticides, and synthetic fibers.

Another case in point is the machine-tool industry, which either turned out too many general-type lathes or too little agricultural machinery. Thus, the distortion of the structure of heavy industry was one of the major factors causing the imbalance between consumption and production.

Finally, to maintain a proper balance between consumption and accumulation, it is imperative to invest the proper proportion among related departments, for whether or not consumption and accumulation maintain a proper balance in the current year hinges on whether or not investment funds were proportionately allocated among the related departments in preceding years. These proportions include allocation of capital funds for productive purposes as well as for non-productive purposes; funds for heavy industry and for light industry; funds to be appropriated among various agricultural departments; and funds for departments within heavy industry that turn out products for its own use and for the departments that support agriculture and light industry. Proportional allocations of capital funds in the current year will directly and indirectly affect consumption and accumulation for future years.

In China, disproportionate allocations of capital funds in certain years aggravated the imbalance between consumption and accumulation. For instance, investment for nonproductive construction, which accounted for 40.2 percent during the First Five-Year Plan, declined to 12.9 percent during the Second Five-Year Plan and to as low as 2.8 percent in 1960. Although an upward adjustment was made in later years, investment for nonproductive construction was never restored to the peak reached during the First Five-Year Plan. It was less than 25 percent for 1971 through 1978 and below 17.1 percent in 1976.

The negligence of investment for nonproductive construction affected the Chinese standard of living. According to a survey of 182 cities in 1978, urban living space per person—because of a housing shortage—declined from 4.5 square meters for 1952 to 3.6 for 1978. In the course of capital construction over the years, investment in heavy industry was too high as compared to investment in agriculture and light industry, thereby distorting the industrial infrastructure and depressing the people's livelihood.

The imbalance between consumption and accumulation brought about by the distorted industrial structure cannot be corrected in a short span of time. It takes time to restructure the economy. In fact, it would take so much capital that China would have difficulty in accumulating it, particularly when the country is trying to scale down the level of construction. Therefore, to rely primarily on domestic resources to carry out capital construction, China must, and foremost, build a balanced industrial structure.

Drawing lessons from the grave mistakes the country has committed over the years of mishandling the relationship between consumption and accumulation, China has, since 1979, been bent on readjusting the ratio between consumption and accumulation, scaling down the latter to a reasonable level, gradually enhancing its efficiency, and rationally allocating funds among departments. To achieve the objectives, China has adopted a series of measures such as a slowdown of the speed in heavy industry; a reduction of investment in capital construction; a raise of workers' wages and peasants' income; a readjustment of the production structure, particularly the composition of heavy industry and a speedup of housing and urban construction; the acceleration of the development of science, culture, education, and public hygiene; a cutback in production costs; raising profits; etc.

After a year's adjustment, the ratio between consumption and accumulation has begun to move in the right direction. Accumulation, which declined to 33.6 percent last year, will probably be 30 percent this year and even lower than that in the future. It is our conviction that the restoration of the balance between consumption and accumulation will ensure a healthy development of the national economy and a rapid improvement in the standard of living.

5
The Current Economic Policies of China

He Jianzhang

My topic is China's current economic policies. There are so many economic policies in the country that I can hardly cover all of them in the allotted time; so I will focus on four areas: (1) policies on the rural economy; (2) policies on the collective economy and individual economy in towns and cities; (3) policies on how to develop comparative advantages, encourage competition, and coordinate economic activities; and (4) price policy.

Policies on the Rural Economy

Over 80 percent of China's population lives in the countryside. Virtually all foodstuffs and approximately 70 percent of the raw materials for light industry come from agriculture, and farm sideline products account for a quarter of the country's total exports. Agricultural performance directly affects the people's livelihood, political stability, industrial development, and foreign trade. Therefore, in readjusting the national economy, of first and foremost importance is the revision of the country's agricultural policy.

It is well known that China's agricultural productivity is low. Although mechanized and semimechanized farming do exist, the bulk of the work in the country is still manual. Under these circumstances, the policy should be flexible; i.e., let the socialist sector of public ownership play a dominant role but, at the same time, allow other economic sectors and different management systems to exist and coexist. China's past errors in this regard lay in the fact that the country

Originally entitled "Xian Jieduan De Zhungguo Jingji Zhengce," this paper was delivered at a seminar held at the Chinese University of Hong Kong, October 1980. He Jianzhang was a member of the Chinese economic delegation that visited Hong Kong.

blindly went after "public ownership" without regard for the level of economic development or the state of the productive forces. China acted as if the greater the scope of collective economy, the better, and the larger the public ownership sector, the better. The country was overhasty in transforming a petty collective economy into a large-scale collective economy, converting the collective economy into public ownership, and eliminating all private economy. Both in formulating and implementing policies, China was not flexible enough to suit the concrete conditions in different localities. Instead, it indiscriminately patted all economic units into a single model. Consequently, the economy was confined to a stereotype that eventually lost its vitality.

During the Cultural Revolution, the Gang of Four preached an unorthodox "heresy" by demanding that the production team, rather than the production brigade, be the basic accounting unit and that all sideline production, including rural fairs and private plots—which were branded as "capitalist legacies"—be either restricted or banned. Under the pretext of opposing material incentive, the Gang of Four discarded all work quotas, threw away the principle of "to each according to his work," and refused to pay the laborer by the work he had done. Instead, they practiced egalitarianism. Such crimes of the Gang of Four gravely dampened the activism of both the collective economy and the peasantry, thereby setting back the country's agricultural development.

To cope with the situation, China has adopted a series of readjustments. First, the scope of a productive team's activities is to be determined by the specific conditions of each individual locality. Those teams that have overextended their activities, those that are too fragmented to effectively carry out collective work, and those that have not run well for a long time should scale down their activities. As for those that have already been transformed into production brigades (large economic operation entities) and for those production brigades that are not doing well, if the majority of their members so wish, they should be allowed to break up into production teams (small operation entities).

Second, the management and operations of the production brigades should be flexible, diversified, lively, and versatile; they should carry out their activities according to the respective conditions, such as endowments and levels of production. They can form year-round operation teams that have set production quotas and are to be paid out of the proceeds of their products, or they can form temporary and seasonal operation teams with fixed production quotas. For those activities such as animal husbandry, fishery, and horticulture that demand high skill, the management and operations should be assigned to special teams and households. As for those few scattered, impoverished production brigades whose production is backward, their members should have only fixed production quotas.

Third, private plots have been restored, and individuals are to be encouraged to raise privately owned livestock and fruit trees in order to promote sideline production and trade fairs. Fourth, the ban has been lifted on production brigades' engaging in agricultural sidelines or industrial processing so as to promote joint operations and industry-agriculture integration.

Fifth, economic independence should be granted to enterprises under collective ownership. The state should no longer set a production quota or planting quota for the production brigade—except in the cases of food grains, cotton, and oilseeds, which are subject to state procurement. Gradually, the quota system should be replaced by contracts. It should be the production brigade that determines what to plant and how to distribute its revenue and surplus above the planned quota and procurement, and the state administration should not interfere with these decisions.

Sixth, the procurement prices of agriculture sidelines should be raised substantially. Last year, state procurement expenditures exceeded the proceeds from sales by 10,000 million yuan, or 13 yuan per peasant. In the future, whenever the economic conditions and the state budget permit, the state should earmark a certain amount of funds every year for subsidizing agricultural sidelines and for adjusting the parity ratios between industrial products and agricultural products.

All the policies mentioned above have been well received by the peasants throughout the country. The rural economy has revived, and a prosperous new look has emerged. This reaction manifests the correctness of our new agricultural policies.

Policies on the Collective Economy and Private Economy in Cities and Towns

Handicrafts and petty trades in cities and towns were transformed into collective economy during the drive for communization in 1955. By the end of 1956, over 90 percent of the handicraft workers had joined cooperatives, thus basically completing the socialist transformation. Between 1958 and 1960, many handicraft cooperatives began to mechanize production and merge into factories. These factories paid their workers' salaries and turned over their profits to the state, which, in turn, set the wage scales and fringe benefits. The general rule was that the wage scales and workers' welfare in the cooperatives should be lower than those in the state-operated enterprises. In effect, the cooperative factories, which assumed no responsibility for profits and losses, differed little from the local state-owned enterprises.

Since the socialist transformation of peddlers and petty stores into the state sector in 1958, there had been few, if any, independent stores. Statistics indicate that up to 1953, there were still 9 million individual private workers, or half of the labor force at that time. By late 1966, there were 2 million, but by the end of 1978, after the ten years' catastrophe, individual private workers had been practically wiped out except for 150,000 survivors.

Experience shows that the elimination of the individual private workers and the reduction of the collective economy was a mistake, for the state sector did not have sufficient funds to replace the economic activities once performed by the cooperatives and the individual private workers. Nor did it have sufficient funds to create jobs for the new entrants into the labor force. A strange phenomenon cropped up: Unemployment and a shortage of products and services existed side by side.

This harsh lesson brought home to us the fact that the collective economy as a mode of production will last for a long time in China. Some people hold the view that after the completion of the socialist transformation, there will be no need for the collective economy. That is wrong because trades such as restaurants, apparel, repairing, and other services use a great deal of manual labor and will serve the people better if they are not centrally controlled. These trades, when voluntarily organized as cooperatives or partnerships and assuming the responsibility for their own profits and losses, will function better than as state enterprises.

Therefore, many economic activities should be operated under collective ownership, thereby creating more jobs. The advantages of collective ownership include a fast turnover, great variety, less demand for capital, and greater flexibility. All of these fit well in the current stage of economic development in China. At present, an energetic development of the collective economy provides the only avenue to building a socialist economy and is the sole course to maintaining full employment.

At this point, our main policies on this regard are as follows.

1. Explore every avenue that may lead to the expansion of production and promote collective economy whenever there is such a need and wherever people demand.

2. Help the broad masses develop a collective economy with diversified activities. For example, Beijing municipality has set up a production-service federation to help unemployed workers start various cooperatives. Street committees, government organs, state-

owned enterprises, and production units of other cities can and should assist the masses in developing collective economic activities.

3. Respect a cooperative's economic independence and explore its functional superiority. A cooperative organized on a voluntary basis should assume the responsibility for its profits and losses and its right to compensate employees according to the work done, to operate by democratic principle, and to produce in response to market demand. The cooperative should have the right to dispose of the means of production and other resources and to make decisions on how to use the proceeds from its economic activities. Under no pretext should the state administration infringe upon the cooperative's property.

4. Abolish irrational regulations that assert that the wage scales and fringe benefits of a cooperative must be lower than those of a state-owned enterprise. A cooperative should have the right to make its own decisions on how to dispose of its income and whether its proceeds are to be distributed according to labor contribution or partly as wages and partly as bonuses. The wage scales of efficient cooperatives can be higher than those of the state-owned enterprises. Other than taxes, no state agencies shall impose levies on cooperatives.

5. A cooperative should be treated on the same basis as a state enterprise. State agencies should provide the cooperatives under their administration with active support in respect to materials and equipment and should pay the cooperatives adequately when they work for state enterprises.

Develop Comparative Advantages, Encourage Competition, and Promote Better Coordination

One of the principal errors of our economic policy in the past was to neglect developing a commodity economy. Every locality sought after autarky, and as a result, there was little interregional trade. This is a petty producer's outlook of a natural economy. It has gravely inhibited the division of labor, the development of a commodity economy, and the exploration of comparative advantages between areas, thus impeding foreign trade.

In the last two years, there has been an expanded experiment in which more power has been delegated to enterprises to make decisions, the market has been assigned a more active role in regulating economic activities, and local governments have acquired some independence in public finance. This policy, however, has posed new problems. On the one hand, enterprises tend to expand their share of the market by breaking up the trade barriers imposed between regions; on the other hand, local governments, worrying about the effect on their revenues, often try to restrict competition between regions and even to deny market access to outsiders. For example, to push the sales of locally produced goods, enterprises and production brigades would be prohibited from purchasing better and less expensive goods produced elsewhere. Some local governments, attempting to raise revenues, ran duplicate projects, made overlapping investments, and even withheld shipments of raw materials to other regions. Obviously, none of these problems is conducive to developing comparative advantages. Nor does the policy conform to the economic principle that calls for maximum output with minimum input. It is for the purpose of redressing the autarky policy of the past and the emerging contradictions of the present that the new policy of "developing comparative advantage" has been put forward. The new policy is to promote competition and improve coordination.

As a rule, every region has its comparative advantages as well as its comparative disadvantages. A correct economic policy should be to produce those goods for which the region has comparative advantages and to not produce, or produce less of, those goods for which the region has comparative disadvantages. To follow this policy, it is necessary to break down trade barriers between regions and to encourage competition. Only through competition can regions reveal their comparative advantages.

An enterprise that pursues the principle of division of labor and produces in large scale can lower costs and win in competition. Thus, competition would compel large and small self-sufficient enterprises to practice division of labor and better coordination. At this very moment, various models of vertical and horizontal integration are under experimentation. The first model pools together all factories producing similar goods into a specialized corporation. For example, the Nanjing Radio Corporation, which manufactures the renowned Panda brand of transistor radios, consists of 38 factories and research institutes. The second model consists of state enterprises incorporated with factories owned by cities or towns or production brigades. The Shanghai Light Industry Bureau, Textile Industry Bureau, and Handicraft Bureau jointly set up 140 different plants in the first half of this year. The third model involves an integration between regions where raw materials are available with regions where the materials are processed. Just last year alone, Shanghai jointly set up twelve projects with various provinces and regions. Engaging in domestic compensation trade, Shanghai provided funds, technology, and equipment, and the provinces and regions furnished lumber, pulp, and other materials.

The fourth model consists of agriculture-industry-commerce jointly operated enterprises; i.e., factories and affiliated stores join with state farms or production brigades to engage in manufacturing, processing, and marketing. They all share profits and losses. Up to now, there are over 100 such enterprises jointly operated by state farms and counties.

The fifth model comprises various types of corporations. Some special districts have set up joint ventures with foreign capital, and experiments of these models of joint operation have revealed that well-coordinated economic activities can develop comparative advantages in different regions and departments and improve economic efficiency. Pooling together regional resources to meet the urgent demand for national construction may help break down mutual exclusiveness between regions and departments, thus enhancing division of labor and avoiding blindly going after overlapping production.

In essence, competition will inevitably lead to vertical and horizontal integration, which is an objective necessity in developing comparative advantages. Hence, economic coordination and integration are natural tendencies in China's economic development.

Price Policy

In the prevailing price system, there are a number of inconsistencies in the relative prices between industry and agriculture, as well as among industrial products. Prices of processed industrial goods tend to be high, and prices of intermediate goods and raw materials are low. In fact, the latter are so low that there is little margin for profit. Although the prices of products using newly introduced inputs are relatively high, the prices of goods using agricultural inputs are relatively low.

This price system, a mixture of exorbitantly high prices and exorbitantly low prices, can hardly regulate production according to social needs, for in this case, there is no incentive to curtail production of the goods that are in excess of demand, nor is there incentive to raise production of the goods that fall short of supply. Under the circumstances, it is difficult to analyze the economic effects of production, investment, and management, nor is the price system conducive to a proper coordination of economic activities between regions and departments. Specifically, it is difficult to accurately assess the social contributions of various industries. In the current experiment, if the retained profit is fixed as a ratio to unit price, it would favor some enterprises while discriminating against others. Certainly, it would dampen the incentives of some enterprises and their workers.

All these difficulties were brought about by our irrational price policy and price system. Under the existing overcentralized price system, an enterprise is deprived of the power to set the prices of its products, and the prices are subject to frequent consultations and approval by the higher state authorities. As a result, the delays and interruptions leave many remaining price problems unsolved.

However, for a long time in the past, we unduly stressed price stability. Many prices were frozen for years, thereby becoming increasingly irrational. Now we will let the market forces regulate economic activities under state guidance. We should encourage competition and open up more trade channels to stimulate production and to meet people's needs. In short, our price system is urgently in need of reform.

The reform must focus on the integration of economic planning and the market. Under the guidance of state planning, enterprises should consciously employ the law of value to set prices. While observing unified price management, it is necessary to be flexible in setting prices. A preliminary outline of the new price policy is given below.

First, the power to set prices should be delegated to the lower levels, which will enable the price control commission and other related departments and ministries of the State Council to concentrate on their primary functions. Those functions are (a) overseeing the implementation of price policies; (b) drafting general guidelines governing price policy and fixing the prices of a few commodities that are essential to the economy or the people's livelihood; and (c) laying down rules procedures regarding the price movements of major commodities, while leaving the prices of other goods to be set by local governments or enterprises.

Second, we will change the uniform price system to a multiprice system: (a) The state will set the prices of only those goods that are essential to the economy or to the people; (b) the state either sets up a ceiling below which prices are allowed to fluctuate or lets prices float within limits of a preset norm; and (c) potential buyers and sellers can negotiate prices, except those of products under state unified purchase. Prices of farm produce and sideline products, as well as those of some industrial products, should also be set through negotiation. When purchasing farm produce above the planned quota, the Department of Commerce should pay the market prices. Prices of commodities marketed in county fairs should be allowed to fluctuate according to market supply and demand and subject to negotiation.

Third, an enterprise should have the power to set and adjust prices. Within the range and scope specified by the higher authorities of the departments concerned, an enterprise should have the right to set and adjust the exfactory, wholesale, and retail prices and to make adjustments for differences in quality, seasonal fluctuations, etc.

There are three overall guiding principles of adjustment. One, the price must reflect the commodity value; i.e., it should be set or adjusted on the basis of the average cost of production under normal conditions. Therefore, the margin of profit in all trades will be approximately the same. Two, production, circulation, and consumption of some commodities are to be regulated through the market price mechanism. And three, prices are subject to political and economic dictations; for example, a high tax rate for high-priced commodities and a low tax rate for low-priced commodities—even tax free or state subsidized if necessary. Let taxation play a role in the price system. It can regulate the distribution of profits between industry and commerce, as well as among industries.

Since the well-being of the state, enterprises, and individuals depends heavily on the price system, adjustments of prices must be carried out energetically and prudently. For prices of the means of production, which do not directly affect the market or people's livelihood, the adjustment should be implemented right away, say, in a year or two. Among the commodities, the prices of coal and lumber—which have a great impact on the economy—should be systematically adjusted. As a matter of fact, such an undertaking is under way.

To improve the people's standard of living over the last decade, the state frequently raised procurement prices of grain, cotton, oilseeds, and other staples while holding the retail prices of those commodities constant, and the subsidies cost the state more than 10,000 million yuan. Before raising the prices of those commodities, China substantially adjusted the wage scales, but that is not easy because the state budget is still in the red. For the years to come, China will continue the subsidies, but it is to be hoped that China will find a permanent solution in due time. In summary, the price policy should promote production and improve the people's standard of living.

6
The Restructuring of the Management of China's Economic System

Liao Jili

My topic is the recent reform of the management of China's economic system. The crux of the reform lies in choosing the proper model to build a socialist economy, and the current economic management system needs a thorough reorganization and readjustment. This great event has not only captured the attention of the Chinese people but also their foreign friends. It is a pleasure to have the opportunity to express my personal view on this issue, and I hope my discussion will throw light on the reform.

Why Reform is Necessary

The necessity for overhauling the management of China's economic system stems from the fact that its existing productive forces are weak and underdeveloped. Over the last thirty years, starting from an extremely poor and backward economy inherited from the old China, we have built a relatively independent and comprehensive industrial base. Today, our economy stands on a fairly solid material base and has great potential for further development. Compared with advanced capitalist countries, however, we are still economically poor and technologically backward.

One of the major causes of the above-mentioned problems is the inadequacy of the management of our economic system. During the First Five-Year Plan period, while productivity was still low and the commodity sector of the economy was underdeveloped, we modeled our system on that prevailing in the Soviet Union during the 1930s and

Originally entitled "Zhungguo Jingji Tizhi Gaige De Xin Jinzhan," this paper was presented at a seminar held at the Chinese University of Hong Kong, October 1980. Liao was a member of the Chinese economic delegation that visited Hong Kong.

1950s. That system is highly centralized and administration oriented. We must admit, however, that at a time when China was just freed from a protracted feudal role and from the Western blockade, when its battered economy still lay in ruins, when technology and productivity were backward and low, and when the social framework was primitive, the economic system did play an important role in pooling together meager resources, funds, and skills and rapidly rehabilitating the devastated economy. This system ensured the smooth implementation of the economic reconstruction, which was centered on 156 core projects.

That system, however, has its drawbacks. It inhibits the development of a commodity economy, minimizes the role of the market price, and tampers with the law of value. We learned how to use the market mechanism to coordinate the economic activities of different economic sectors during the First Five-Year Plan period, but after the completion of the socialist transformation, we overstressed centralization and neglected the role of the market. As a result, a number of shortcomings gradually emerged, including rigid state control and inflexibility. Because of the sabotages of Lin Biao and the Gang of Four, there has been no profound reform of the system in the last two decades. On the contrary, the system has grown more and more petrified and incompatible with the development of the productive forces.

Among others, the system has four major drawbacks. First, the enterprise is treated as an appendage of various ministries and departments, which is incompatible with the development of a socialist commodity economy. Second, the intrinsic economic interrelations and interdependence among industries and regions are arbitrarily broken down and replaced by administrative relations. This is inconsistent with the socialist system of large-scale production. Third, the plan targets handed down from above are too rigid to accommodate actual demand or to cope with the complex and ever-changing social needs. Fourth, the practice of unified procurement and fixed state supplies, and the "iron rice bowl" job system, are inconsistent with the economic principle that calls for maximum results with minimum effort. Rather, the economic system creates too many redundant apparatuses, duplicate procedures, bad coordination between regions, red tape, and inaction. It breeds bureaucracy and waste of manpower, resources, and funds; it gravely inhibits the advancement of technology and the elevation of productivity and impairs the development of socialist superiority.

Since the smash of the Gang of Four, with the shift of our Party line to socialist modernization, we have accorded top priority to streamlining the economy. An overhaul of the system is imminent. Just as we can reform our political system, so can we reform our economic system. The agenda of the reform is as follows.

First, smash the shackles that once fettered our people's minds. It is now feasible to draw realistic positive and negative lessons from the experience acquired during the past thirty years. We will set straight our ideology, correct our Party line, and reexamine the laws governing the development of socialism. Second, the periodic outbreaks of political movement are over. Now the country is united and stable, so we are in a position to concentrate on economic reform. Third, as the reform is proceeding favorably, the imbalances among economic sectors are being corrected and industrial and agricultural production are steadily rising. Fourth, China has abandoned its seclusion policy and is drawing on foreign experience as a reference in carrying out its own economic development. In a few years and step by step, China can restructure its economy to accommodate the needs of the socialist modernization.

What Is the Direction of the Reform?

Just as economic and social conditions vary from country to country, so do management systems. Economic reforms in China must proceed from the vantage point of developing China's productive forces and in the light of the characteristics of its socialist economy. To set the direction of the reform, we should focus on some major issues facing the economy and then draw on the experiences of foreign countries.

The salient features of the Chinese economy are its massive land, overgrown population, weak industrial foundation, low productivity, backward technology, imbalances among economic sectors, underdeveloped commodity production, and poor transportation and communication facilities. Because of this state of affairs, our reform should focus primarily on the development of that part of the commodity economy in which the state sector is to play a dominant role while coexisting with the other sectors, which include the enterprises and the toiling masses.

To run such a system, one should integrate economic planning with the market; i.e., rely primarily on the economic machinery and economic means to serve genuinely the interests of the state, of the collectives, and of the broad masses. For such a reform, an enterprise should be free from rigid state control and be treated as an independent economic entity, which assumes the responsibility for profits and losses. Enterprises should carry out their activities according to social needs and the guidelines laid down in state plans.

Second, national, regional, and interregional economic organizations should be set up according to the principles of division of labor and industrial interdependence. This will improve the shortcomings in the current economic system, in which enterprises are mutually exclusive, fragmented, and poorly coordinated. Third, China should expand the sector of commodity production and circulation and establish a unified market in which capital goods and consumer goods will be traded as commodities, except for a few necessities that will be rationed according to state plans.

Fourth, economic and trade centers should be set up where activities will be carried out according to intrinsic industrial interdependence, which is dictated by expanded social reproduction rather than according to administrative functions or geographical distribution. Fifth, China should reverse the existing planning practice that arbitrarily imposes production targets from the top and replace it with a planning system that integrates both the upper and the lower levels. Mandatory directives should be tempered by flexible guidelines.

Sixth, instead of relying on administrative control, China should use prices, taxation, monetary policy, and other means to regulate economic activities. Seventh, work discipline should be strictly enforced, economic legislation strengthened, and supervision tightened. Eighth, the Party and the state organs should be relieved of their routine functions so they can focus on policies. Leave the operations and the decision making to the enterprises with no Party or state interference.

Ninth, state control should be relaxed and some of the economic power should be delegated to regions, which, under state unified leadership, are to be responsible for planning, implementing, and supervising economic activities. Tenth, the factory manager should be responsible to the workers' congress rather than to factory Party committees.

The above-mentioned factors constitute an organic whole. If and when they are incorporated and carried out in the reform, the economic system will encompass both the virtues of socialist planning and the merits of a market economy, for it will be primarily a centralized system and yet have no rigid control. Such a system can develop a socialist commodity economy and enhance the socialist productive forces.

Progress Made in the Reform

Based on the extensive studies, we have launched an economic reform. Its essential factors are summed up as follows.

1. In an expanded pilot experiment, we have delegated decision-making power to many enterprises. Up to the first half of this year, the experiment has covered approximately 6,000 enterprises whose products accounted for 45 percent of the gross value of industrial product in the public sector of the economy. Having acquired new capacities of production and distribution, the enterprises began emerging as independent economic entities. The experiment has been a great driving force in arousing the activism of the broad masses, in boosting production, and in improving management. According to the statistics of 84 local enterprises in Sichuan Province, the output value for 1979 rose 14.9 percent compared to last year's profit of 33 percent. Of the profits, 24.2 percent were turned over to the state. For the first half of this year, the value of industrial output in Shanghai rose 8.5 percent, and the profit turned over to the state was 5.3 percent, of which the output value of the pilot textile mills rose 14.1 percent, and the profit turned over to the state was 16.3 percent compared to the same period last year.

2. Since the reinstatement of the market under state guidelines, the means of production traded as commodities have gradually found their way to the market, and more channels have opened up for consumer goods. In the past, capital goods were produced and distributed according to state plans; now they are freely produced and marketed after the planned target has been fulfilled.

For example, the more than 20 million tons of steel products turned out in 1979 were over and above the planned target and sold in the market. Likewise, 5 billion yuan of machinery was produced by the First Machinery Ministry in response to market demand, which was equivalent to 14 percent of the value of the ministry's total output. Besides, the production plans of most enterprises under state administration were drawn up in conformity with contract specifications. Preliminary statistics reveal that of the 210 models of machinery and electric appliances under state unified distribution, 146, or 69 percent, are freely marketed now. In 1979 alone, there were 600 new enterprises and 60 new trade centers that manufactured, marketed, and shipped capital goods for other enterprises. It is estimated that goods worth over 3.5 billion yuan were traded. These enterprises were even more active in producing and marketing consumer goods. According to the preliminary statistics, over 35 percent of the consumer goods were produced for and channeled through the market.

3. A new public finance system has been put into effect recently, according to which the state and the local governments must delineate their respective revenues and expenditures, as well as their allocation

of investment funds. This delineation of financial responsibilities between different levels of administration, together with the profits retention incentive, have aroused the enthusiasm of both enterprises and local governments, cut down expenditures, and raised revenues. From January through June of this year, the revenues of local governments reached 36 billion yuan, or 6 percent over last year, and expenditures declined to 23 billion yuan, or 10 percent below last year. The favorable development stems from separating the financial management of the different levels of administration and from retrenching expenditures while augmenting revenue. Many local governments took the initiative and transformed or closed down enterprises that had long incurred losses. All these improvements have strengthened financial management and enhanced the reform.

4. Some enterprises have begun to specialize while maintaining coordination with various affiliated factories and the head office. In keeping with the principle of division of labor, a number of provinces and cities have formed specialized corporations and multifunction enterprises. Statistics from seventeen provinces and cities indicate that since 1979, over 1,000 specialized corporations have been established. In some areas, joint operations and compensation trade have been organized between localities, as well as between state enterprises and collectives and between urban enterprises and rural communes. This change has not only improved economic efficiency, it has also fully tapped the potentials of individual enterprises.

In 1979, Shanghai's handicraft industry set up six multiproduct factories to manufacture sport shoes, electric irons, etc. As a result of the integrated specialization, production rose sharply. Output increased 50 percent above last year, and the number of electric irons produced soared 34 percent. In rural areas, over 100 state farms have set up agriculture-industry jointly operated enterprises.

5. On a trial basis, capital construction will be financed by bank loans rather than by free state appropriation. Construction projects in the experiment include light industry, textiles, coal, power, petroleum, transportation, building materials, commerce, tourism, etc. Up to the end of last June, a total credit of 2 billion yuan had been extended to light industry, textiles, railroads, transportation, metallurgy, petroleum, commerce, and other industries for short- and intermediate-term innovation and remodeling.

In the past, funds for capital construction were directly appropriated by the state, and neither the appropriating department nor the recipient department was responsible for profits or losses. As capital funds were freed, local governments and enterprises used to compete for more funds, but they paid little attention to economizing in using the capital. Now, since investments are financed by bank loans, capital efficiency has been enhanced, and enterprises that borrow from banks are subject to the latter's supervision and auditing. For instance, the Shanghai Non-Ferrous Rolling Metal Works, with a planned annual processing capacity of 10,000 tons of copper, applied for 6.85 million yuan to expand its capacity to 40,000 tons—the amount applied for was three times over actual need. When bank loans replaced free state appropriations, the steel mill manager, worrying about the cost of the loan, took merely 2 million yuan. The planned capacity was met by technical innovations and a better utilization of the existing facilities.

6. Multitrade models have been developed and resources of different economic sectors have been pooled. Agricultural policy has been liberalized to suit the conditions of individual localities, especially the poor, remote mountainous areas where production quotas were formerly fixed down to the production team or even to the individual household. Individual private economy is now permissible. Collectively owned handicrafts, retail stores, restaurants, repair shops, and transportation and construction teams have been revived in cities. Besides, the reinstatement of individual handicraftsmen and peddlers created many jobs, enlivened the market, and improved the people's livelihood.

In 1979, over 9 million new jobs were created, of which collectively owned enterprises accounted for 4 million, or 44 percent of the total new jobs. In the first half of 1980, over 4 million new jobs were created, of which collectively owned enterprises accounted for 1 million, or 32 percent of the total. When the republic was first founded, there were 9 million self-employed workers, of which 2 million survived in 1966, but by 1978, there were fewer than 150,000. After the reform, however, the number increased to 320,000 in 1979 and 330,000 up to May of this year.

In short, although the experiment started just recently, it has already broken loose the shackles of the existing economic system, aroused the activism and initiative of people in many localities, and motivated enterprises and workers to improve management and increase production. It has achieved favorable economic results, revived the whole economy, and paved the way for further reform.

What to Do in the Immediate Future

A comprehensive overhaul of the economic management system is an intricate and complex task. Chinese and foreign experiences suggest that reforms can be carried out step by step only when the conditions are ripe. The current reform, which may last several years, should not be hastened because few things can be accomplished overnight.

There were two extensive and far-reaching reforms in China in 1958 and 1970, respectively, but neither achieved satisfactory results. One of the reasons for the failure was a lack of preparation and planning. The old system had been cast away before the new ones were hastily put into effect. History witnesses that a successful reform calls for great resolution, clear direction, good coordination, and phased progress in the right order of sequence. At present, the economic reform in China has entered upon a crucial transition period. We should promptly set forth the objective of the reform and the means to achieve it and then persistently and consistently push the reform forward. The objectives of our reform for the immediate future are as follows.

1. We shall continue improving the initial reforms. A major issue is how to coordinate the new measures, which have already been put under way for further development. So far, the experiment has been confined to delegating decision-making powers to the enterprises, primarily the power of disposing of a portion of the earned profits. From now on, an enterprise should be allowed to draft its own plans, market its products, and purchase materials and equipment, as well as to develop horizontal and vertical coordinations with other enterprises.

To further develop the restructured and reoriented enterprises in light of the reform policy, it is necessary to create jointly operated enterprises and to encourage trades such as handicrafts, restaurants, repair shops, and other services, whether under collective ownership or private ownership. Correspondingly, we should open up more channels of circulation for both capital and consumer goods according to market supply and demand. Some of these goods are under state uniform purchase and sale, some under planned trade, some under preferential treatment, and others are to be freely traded.

2. We should stress reforms of the price system and fiscal and monetary policies, so that as economic leverages, they will genuinely perform their regulatory functions. First of all, the prices of the means of production call for extensive readjustment. For example, some enterprises earned profits because of efficient management, but other profits were incurred as a result of irrational state pricing. To remove the cause of the unfair distribution of profits between enterprises and to encourage competition, we may have to operate a multitier price system.

On fiscal policy, instead of continuing the current practice that requires enterprises to turn over their revenues to the state, we will systematically replace it by profit taxes. This change will not only assure an enterprise a reasonable return on investment under normal conditions, but also provide the state and local governments with a steady and reliable flow of revenue.

In a planned way, we should let banks finance an enterprise's capital investment, instead of the present direct allocation of construction funds and working capital by the state free of cost. In that case, banks would perform some functions of economic regulation.

With respect to employment, we should adopt every measure feasible to create jobs, which includes projects to be organized by labor unions or labor departments, as well as by self-employed individuals. Within the framework of the state manpower plan, enterprises should be allowed to freely recruit employees through competition.

3. We should strengthen state planning. With the expansion of a horizontal coordination of economic activities, a mandatory fulfillment of planned targets will be reduced, but planning as a guide for economic activities is to be strengthened, for to meet the demand of socialized large-scale production, to ensure proportional growth among various sectors of the economy, and to prevent anarchy in production and construction, it is necessary to stress state planning. The state should focus its attention primarily on important objects, such as attaining comprehensive and overall balance in long-range plans, setting priorities for major construction projects, defining the scope and scale of capital investment, maintaining an adequate ratio among the different sectors of the economy, and raising the people's standard of living.

In drafting short-term annual plans, we should stress four principal balances: namely, state budget, material supplies, bank credit, and foreign exchange. Using various economic measures, the state should provide guidance to enterprises so that they can carry out their activities within the planned framework.

Once a long-range plan is drawn up, individual enterprises can each work out its annual plan on a contractual basis, from lower levels all the way to the top; striking a balance on every level and reaching out for vertical integration. This system will certainly lead to a better integration between economic planning and the market.

4. Simultaneously, we should strengthen our statistical system, set up information centers, compile data banks, and make economic forecasts. Moreover, we should establish adequate machinery to better coordinate economic activities. All these aids are bound to strengthen, expand, and improve our economic planning.

7
Relationship Between Planning and the Market Under Socialism

Liu Guoguang
Zhao Renwei

Integration of Planning and the Market

For quite some time, there has been a view prevailing in the socialist countries that planning in a socialist economy is incompatible with the market in a capitalist economy. In recent years, although the people have gradually accepted the view that commodity production and the law of value still operate in a socialist economy, economic planning and the market have been treated as being mutually exclusive, as if there were no place for the market in a planned economy, nor could economic planning exist in a market economy. Such a view has brought a series of disasters to our economy.

Deviation of Production from Demand

Because of the one-sided emphasis on planning at the neglect of the market, the problems of what to produce and how to produce are arbitrarily fixed by high state officials and imposed on the enterprises. Consequently, production has not been geared to social needs. So, what has been produced found no demand, and what has been in demand found no supply. Moreover, most of the goods produced by the enterprises were regulated under state unified procurement and marketing, and the bulk of the means of production was also under state unified supply and planned allocation. There was little coordination between the consumers and the producer and no direct face-to-face contact. As a result, the producers had no idea what the consumer

A slightly abridged version of a paper first published in *Economic Research*, no. 5 (1979), pp. 46–55, with the title "Guanyu Shehuizhuyi Jingjizhung Jihua Yu Shichang De Guanxi Wenti." It has also been published in *Red Flag*, no. 9 (1979), and *Atlantic Economic Journal* 7:4 (1979), pp. 11–21.

needed, nor could the consumer exert any influence on production. Therefore, the disparity between the planned targets and the actual needs could not be properly reflected in the market, and the long-standing disequilibria among production, supply, and distribution could not be restored.

Disparity Between Planned Price and Cost

Since there were no objective criteria to determine the value of a product, the planned prices of many products deviated from their values by a wide margin. Without a criterion to determine the value of a product—and thereby the profit—it would be difficult to evaluate an enterprise's performance. The profits and losses brought about by irrational pricing cannot be used to assess economic results. In the past, market supply and demand were rarely taken into consideration in fixing price.

When commodities fell short of demand, instead of adjusting prices so as to raise supply and discourage demand, coupons were issued. Thus, coupons took over the functions of money and created a multivalue system. Some people call this "planned supply" and regard it as a feature of a socialist economy. What they do not know is that the suppression of demand by coupons has nothing to do with socialism. To be sure, under certain conditions within a period of time, a socialist economy can impose quotas or fix prices to regulate supply and demand. Such regulations, however, cannot stimulate the production of commodities that are short in supply. Rather, such regulations often further aggravate production, thus reducing the supply. So, the suppression of demand by coupon cannot fundamentally restore the disequilibrium between supply and demand, but can worsen it.

Fixed Supply of Investment Fund

The role of the market was ignored not only in production, marketing, and allocation of funds, but also in the collection of revenues. In the past, practically all enterprise revenues, profits, and depreciation funds were entirely turned over to the state. In return, the state provided the enterprises, free of charge, all fixed assets and working capital. The enterprises were not held economically responsible for efficient utilization of the assets and funds. As the enterprises were not responsible for the profits and losses, economic accounting became a mechanical bookkeeping and auditing procedure rather than a device that can motivate people to be interested in raising productivity. Under this situation, despite repeated administrative directives and appeals, the enterprises and their employees made little effort to meet the consumers' demands by reducing costs, improving quality, and increasing the varieties. Up to this date, wastes and inaction cannot be eliminated.

Tendency of Autarky

The socialist economy is based on large-scale production, which involves many departments and regions. With the advent of science and technology, specialization of production is bound to take place in a socialist economy. However, owing to the ignorance of the market and to the backwardness of the petty mode of production, the enterprises were driven to self-sufficiency instead of specialization. As a result, the practice of "small and complete" and "large and complete" became commonplace in China. True, the enterprises were not to be blamed for such a state of affairs; it was due to a host of external factors. For instance, the imbalances in production, supply, and marketing and the frequent failures of other enterprises to drive for autarky. From the entire economy's viewpoint, the autarky tendency can be attributed to the neglect of the market.

We should point out that the notion that planning and the market are irreconcilable in a socialist economy is totally groundless in theory as well as in practice. Indeed, a socialist economy based on public ownership is operated according to state plans, but that does not mean it must sever all its relations with the market. What the socialist economy opposes is anarchy—the characteristic of an economy based on private ownership.

What is incompatible with the market is not the planned economy but the natural economy. In the natural economy, there is no commodity-money relationship but a system of distribution in kind. This is one of the basic features of all economies in which production is carried out in a state of anarchy and isolation. Production relations in a market economy are built on the basis of a social division of labor and coordination. Whether or not the market economy is spontaneous and anarchical depends on the system of ownership. With socialist public ownership, market production can be put under the people's conscious control and serve the socialist planned economy.

Inasmuch as market production is based on the socialist division of labor, one can say, at least on this point, that it is not incompatible with the socialist planned economy, which is built on socialized large-scale production. Rather, economic planning and market production have something in common. The socialist planned economy existing under the conditions of commodity production relations uses money as the medium of exchange. As such, it is incompatible with the natural economy and spontaneous economy, but not with the market production economy under the people's conscious control.

In the past, the reasons that some people stressed only planning to the neglect of the market can be attributed to two traditional misconceptions. One attempted to equate the market with spontaneous production, particularly the anarchy under capitalism; the other mixed up the planned economy with the natural economy. Some people often used the former as an argument to oppose the market. Whoever speaks of utilizing the market mechanism would be branded as going capitalist. The latter has become a theoretical contest that confuses the socialist economy with the natural economy. Under the protection of the two traditional misconceptions and misled by the catchwords—resolutely upholding the socialist planned economy and opposing the capitalist market economy—many irregularities and malpractices, which have nothing to do with socialism, flourished.

The economy was managed by simple administrative directives instead of economic laws. Work was done according to senior officials' subjective wishes rather than objective laws. Paternalism replaced the rule of democracy. Feudalism and bureaucratic management, which might be workable for a natural economy, are no substitute for scientific management for large-scale socialist production. In a country where 80 percent of the people are peasants and where commodity production is still underdeveloped, the concepts and practices of self-sufficiency are deeply rooted in its social fibers.

At the present stage, when the two systems of ownership coexist, we think the commodity-money productive relations are quite important for our economic development, particularly when the bulk of the population consists of peasants and collective ownership still plays a dominant role in agricultural production. The role of commodity-money productive relations between the two systems of ownership should be all the more respected, but to explain why the commodity-money productive relations and the market are compatible in the socialist system by simply pointing to the fact that they do coexist fails to grasp the essence of the issue. In effect, such a view implies that the role of the commodity is inconsistent with the ownership of the whole people, for although the view may be able to explain that the coexistence of the commodity-money productive relations and the market is brought about by exogenous factors, it cannot explain why there are intrinsic factors in the ownership of the whole people that must give rise to the coexistence of the commodity-money productive relations and the market.

In Chinese economist circles, several views have prevailed that are actually derived from the above-mentioned "external factor theory." Those views include "facadism," which refers to the fact that the means of production distributed in the system of the ownership by the whole people are no longer commodities; "substitutism," which maintains that the law of value is to be replaced by the planned and proportionate development of the national economy; and "instrumentalism," which holds that the law of value and the value-related economic leverages—such as price, profit, cost, interest, etc.—are no longer regulators but simply dispensable accounting tools.

The existence of the commodity-money productive relations in the system of the ownership by the whole people is believed to be determined by the material interests that exist during the stage of socialism. Under the system of public ownership of the means of production, the antagonism between the exploiter and the exploited has been eliminated. However, during the stage of socialism, labor has not yet become a spontaneous social obligation but is merely a means of subsistence. As people differ in ability and contribution, there will be differences in material compensations.

The differences in material interest are manifested not only among people but also among enterprises in the same system of ownership by the whole people. When the differences in production performances among enterprises are brought about not by external factors but by their subjective efforts, the material compensations to the enterprises and their staffs and workers would have to be different; otherwise, production would be impeded. Therefore, the economic relationships among various enterprises (which are independent entities) in the system of ownership by the whole people must observe the principle of trade and compensation on the basis of equal value.

Any disregard of this principle is a denial of the people's differences in material interest and thereby ignores their material interests. This specific role of material interest under socialism is the direct cause of the existence of commodity-money productive relations—of course, material interests are based on the division of labor and socialized production. Such a commodity relationship, or market production relationship, is deeply entrenched in the differences between people's material interests. It is neither an objective reality nor an economic mechanism. Here one must realize that the so-called direct social labor of ownership by the whole people refers to the relations between individual labor and social labor that are free of the handicaps of the spontaneous markets of private ownership. In fact, during the stage of socialism, exchange between laborers, as well as between enterprises, must observe the principle of trading on equal value; therefore, the direct social labor can only be realized through a planned market. In other words, a planned distribution and conservation of social labor can only be realized through the market mechanism, which manifests a specific material interest relation under socialism.

Clearly, the relationship between planning and the market under socialism is neither mutually exclusive nor completely integrated by external forces. Rather, it is an internal organic integration determined by the very nature of a socialist economy. If it is the integration of the people's material interests under ownership of the whole people that created the material conditions for planned management, then the above-mentioned differences in the people's material interests are the immediate causes of the existence of the market in a socialist economy. The consistency or inconsistency of the people's material interests under socialism is precisely the objective condition by which the contradictions between planning and the market in a socialist economy can be synthesized.

How to Utilize the Market Mechanism in a Socialist Economy

Development of commodity production and utilization of the market mechanism cannot be carried out independently of the commodity producers' economic activities in the market. Apart from enterprises under collective ownership, the primary component of the socialist market consists of enterprises under ownership by the whole people (some countries have socialized ownership). These enterprises sell to, as well as purchase from, the market all kinds of means of production and of consumption. To exercise the market functions, enterprises under ownership by the whole people must have the right to make economic decisions and be treated as independent commodity producers. If enterprises under ownership by the whole people were deprived of all rights and responsibilities, it would be meaningless to say that they made use of the market mechanism. Therefore, the issue of utilizing the market is intimately associated with that of extending the enterprises' right of management.

Under socialism, the market mechanism must rely on the economic leverages and economic machinery—including price, costs, interest, and taxes, which are all related to the law of value—so as to tie an enterprise's performance to its material interests. This reliance is the essence of making use of economic means to run an economy. Should one fail to pay attention to the economic leverages and to the material interests of the individuals and enterprises, and rely solely on administrative methods to run an economy, then there is no need to talk about utilization of the market. Therefore, all these issues are closely related to the problem of running an economy by economic means.

In short, to make use of the market mechanism, it is necessary to link it with the extension of an enterprise's economic rights and with the employment of economic means to run the economy. All these requirements are for the purpose of achieving a rational allocation and effective utilization of materials, funds, and manpower according to social needs. But how can the market mechanism, the extension of the enterprise's right of management, and the use of economic means allocate manpower, materials, and funds?

Allocate Resources So That Production Is Determined by Supply and Demand

What commodities shall an enterprise produce and in what quantities? What are the rules governing an enterprise's marketing of its products? Where do enterprises get their resources? The previously mentioned method of production and marketing often resulted in a dislocation between social production and social needs and in a failure to fulfill production goals. We know the goal of socialist production is to meet social needs, and the problems of what to produce and how much are determined by social needs. This is the basic principle of a socialist economy. As a rule, the enterprises produce according to the state plans and according to social needs, but in practice, there are contradictions between the two, for the state plans can only reflect the needs of society in general, not in specifics. Nor can the state plans take into consideration the concrete conditions of every enterprise. Therefore, the quantity, quality, and variety of commodities to be produced by an enterprise should be determined by the specific market demand and the interests of the enterprise instead of being confined exclusively to the targets set by the higher authorities.

Correspondingly, the practices that allow the commerce departments to purchase and market capital goods and consumer goods regardless of whether or not there is demand for them must be ended. Except for a few goods that are in short supply, all goods should be distributed by the market. Gradually, consumer goods are to be marketed by the producing enterprise directly so as to meet the demand, and the producers' goods are to be treated as commodities. Producers and state procurement agencies should have direct contact, and their transactions are to be regulated by contracts rather than by administrative directives.

The strengthening of the market mechanism to solve some of the production and marketing problems lies essentially in reducing costs and increasing variety, in improving quality and augmenting quantity, in removing shortage and eliminating surplus, as well as in enhancing the producers' interests and the consumers' rights.

Allocate Resources According to Economic Results; Make Enterprises Responsible for Profits and Losses

To date, our policy on the allocation of funds has been essentially based on a fixed supply of capital with little market regulation. Inadvertently, that situation tends to motivate enterprises to compete for resources, funds, and foreign exchange, and it impedes the enhancement of investment efficiency and undermines the practice of economic accounting. To rectify this state of affairs, we must change the present system of unified allocation of funds. Let the enterprises be responsible for their own profits and losses, and let the banks take care of loans.

One way in which an enterprise can be responsible for its profits and losses is to allow it to keep a portion of its earned profits for expansion of production, raising the employees' pay, or improving the workers' fringe benefits. However, this retention should be allowed after the enterprise has paid taxes, interests, and loans. During the transition, an enterprise that has fulfilled its financial obligations should be allowed to retain a portion of its earned profits, which can be used to enhance work incentive, to allow technical innovation, or to expand productive facilities. Together with the depreciation allowance and maintenance funds, the enterprise can innovate, renovate, and expand production.

To shift the policy from a free appropriation of funds to bank loans with compensation, the state should levy a rental tax on an enterprise's fixed assets, which are purchased with state funds. Such a tax—compensation for using state capital—together with the retained profits would enable those enterprises that utilize their funds efficiently and operate their businesses successfully to earn profits and accumulate reserves and thus increase their material interests. The reformed system, if implemented, would motivate an enterprise and its employees to tap their potential and to fully utilize capital funds.

When the practice of an enterprise's managing its own finances is well established, we should consider how to let bank loans and the enterprise's retained profits gradually replace the state appropriations of construction funds and working capital. Obviously, the enterprise will be more prudent, more economical, and less cavalier in using the funds when it is responsible for its profits and losses than when the funds are appropriated free of compensation. Now, the enterprise will be permitted to retain a portion of its earned profits after having repaid the loan plus interest. In making loans for capital construction or working capital, the banks should exercise discretion in fixing the interest rates. At the same time, the banks should watch the results of investments and grant loans on a selective basis.

Place Employment on a Competitive Basis;
Allow Free Choice of Jobs Within Limits;
Let Supply and Demand Solve Labor Problems

In the past, among the allocation of labor, financial, and material resources, allocation of labor was furthest from the market mechanism. Although the allocation of laborers to various departments was meted out according to the state plans, the simplistic approach was cumbersome and created numerous problems, for often an enterprise could not hire the worker it needed and the individual could not choose a job that suited his talents. Who would get what job was determined by government officials. Apparently, this system was not a rational way to use labor, raise enthusiasm, improve economic accounting, or achieve better results.

In our opinion, to eliminate the misallocation and the misuse of labor, we should select the person best suited for the job and integrate planned assignment with free choice of employment. Within the limits set by state regulations, an enterprise should have the right to hire the applicant best suited for the job. Likewise, an enterprise should have the right to reassign surplus laborers to wherever they are needed. During the transition, the employees' living allowances should be drawn from the social insurance funds, and an individual should have the freedom to choose his own occupation whenever feasible.

To be sure, free choice of occupation by individuals should by no means be construed as free movement from one enterprise to another, from one department to another, or between rural and urban areas without any control. Free choice of occupation is an essential component of the free development of an individual. As the founder of the scientific socialism put it, the freedom of individuals is a condition of all people's free development.

During the stage of socialism, particularly when the productive forces are still underdeveloped, uncontrolled free choice of occupations is not feasible—as it is possible under communism. Nevertheless, socialism considers working an inherited privilege. Under the present condition of "to each according to his work," when the worker's family more or less, directly or indirectly, pays the expenses of education and training, we should, within limits, grant individuals the right to choose their occupations. This policy conforms to the principle of "to each according to his work and from each according to his ability," provides the individual a better way to explore his talents, and allows society to develop at a faster rate.

Clearly, limited freedom in choosing one's occupation does not imply undisciplined movements of laborers between enterprises and departments or between rural and urban areas. Regulations of labor movements should rely primarily on economic measures and ideological education rather than on administrative and legislative measures. For instance, to encourage workers to stay on a job, a bonus may be granted for seniority; to induce workers to emigrate to remote areas or to take hard jobs, living allowances or wage differentials may be used.

We have dealt with the problems of how to use the market mechanism in a socialist planned economy of commodity production to allocate resources and market goods and to make the best use of labor. The use of the market mechanism to regulate economic activities involves two important factors: price and competition. We will discuss briefly these two factors in the following.

On Price

The regulatory functions of the law of value in socialist production has long been denied in China. Some people who champion constant prices try to equate stable planned prices with long-range frozen prices, but ever-changing economic activities cause frequent variations in factors that affect prices. Any arbitrary freezing of prices will run counter to objective law, causing prices to drift further and further away from reality. For instance, changes in labor productivity would change the value of a product, and productivity is the basic factor that determines price. The rates of change in labor productivity vary from industry to industry, and in general, labor productivity changes faster in industry than in agriculture.

The current disparity between the prices of industrial products and agricultural products is not due entirely to historical factors. As labor productivity rises faster in industry than in agriculture, the disparity between the two would widen if their prices were to remain the same. Take another example: Supply and demand are the major factors that affect commodity price. If prices were frozen, there would be no way that they could reflect changes in supply and demand, which is why the supply and demand of many products were out of equilibrium in China. The state subsidizes those products whose prices are set below costs. Although the maintenance of a stable price level for a period of time may assure steady production and consumption, it can be detrimental, if prolonged, to production, for price control can suppress the symptom but not the disease. Only through an expansion of production can the equilibrium between supply and demand be restored.

In the past, we paid an exorbitant price to maintain price stability. What numerous coupons and queues brought us was nothing but forced equilibrium at the cost of lowering the standard of living. Whenever a commodity is rationed or put under state control, its supply falls even more than if there were no ration. Rations dampen the incentive to increase production. Massive evidence has verified the fact that when prices are irrational, it is difficult to fulfill planned targets. At present, the prices of many commodities have drifted further and further away from their value. These disparities have already adversely affected our economic development—particularly of agriculture, raw materials, and fuel.

To improve the situation in light of the spirit of the Third Plenary Session of the Eleventh Central Committee, price disparities between agriculture and industry have been narrowed, the relative prices of some major products have been adjusted, and enterprises are allowed to vary within limits of the planned prices. The critical question is whether or not we admit that price is a means of market regulation. If prices are allowed to fluctuate within a certain range, then supply and demand can perform the regulatory functions, thus stimulating production. This is precisely how the market mechanism should function under state guidance. Of course, allowing price variations should not be construed as condoning anarchy. In fact, price variations should not be allowed to deviate beyond the planned range. Consumer goods, which are essential to the masses, and the means of production, which affect the costs of major production, should be put under state control for a limited period of time.

Free Competition

As long as a commodity economy prevails, there is competition. To a certain extent, competition and free price movement are interrelated and interdependent, together constituting an organic block of the market mechanism. Without price differentiation, there is no competition; conversely, without competition, there is no price variation, no market regulation, and no operation of the law of value. That production and marketing should be carried out according to market demand, that capital funds should be allocated according to investment returns, and that workers should be hired according to their abilities all hinge on competition.

Usually, people tend to link competition with capitalism, but in effect, competition is not confined exclusively to capitalism. Rather, it is a characteristic that exists in all commodity economies. As commodity production and commodity trade do exist under socialism, precluding competition would be tantamount to denying the existence of the commodity economy. Enterprises under socialism should operate as commodity producers, for whether or not the quality and variety of a commodity are popular and whether the labor consumed in its production is above or below the socially necessary norm will affect the material interests of the people concerned. Competition between enterprises would certainly stimulate technology innovation, improve management, reduce costs, raise productivity, increase the variety, and enhance quality. So, competition will test an enterprise's efficiency and press an enterprise to satisfy the consumers' demand for better goods and greater variety, thus fostering the development of the productive forces.

To be sure, there are fundamental differences between competition under socialism and competition under capitalism. One of the basic differences is that competition in the former is based on public ownership, in which the enterprises share common interests, and competition in the latter is based on private ownership, in which the enterprises have conflicting interests. As socialist competition is not mutually exclusive, it will not lead to anarchy or a polarization of the rich and the poor.

There are differences as well as similarities between socialist emulation and capitalist competition. The similarities lie in that they both tend to push the laggard to catch up with the advanced and to exhort the advanced to make further advancement. Socialist emulation, however, does not involve material incentives, nor the elimination of faltering enterprises, whereas capitalist competition is closely related to material interests and even to the survival of an enterprise. To minimize social losses, the enterprises that cannot produce commodities to meet the market demand, or that incur losses because of factors beyond their control, should suspend operation or be converted to another product. More than that, the state should investigate who is responsible for the losses, and the labor departments should find jobs for the laid-off workers. Unlike capitalism, there is no involuntary unemployment when an enterprise goes out of business.

All in all, the market can play an active and broad role in a socialist planned economy—in production as well as in marketing, in the appropriation of funds as well as in the allocation of manpower. The market mechanism can work well in these and other areas. To do so, however, it is necessary to confine price variations within the planned range. A flexible price, when properly set, is conducive to the realization of plan targets and to a rational and effective use of resources.

Use the Market to Strengthen Economic Planning

In the course of building China's socialist economy, the market mechanism has long been ignored. There is a tendency to deny the usefulness of the market as a means to develop the socialist planned economy, and the fallacy of such a view, if left unexposed, will prevent the market from playing a positive role and hinder the integration of economic planning and the market. Moreover, there is another tendency we oppose, i.e., the exaggeration of the functions of the market at the expense of planning. This tendency seems to have appeared in China and abroad. For instance, some people equate planned economy with bureaucracy, some confuse planned management with running the enterprises by administrative directives, and others look upon planned economy with contempt. At this juncture, when we are reexamining the role of the market in the socialist economy, we must guard against such a tendency.

We should strive to develop socialist commodity production by using the market mechanism. After all, our economy is not one of laissez-faire, and we cannot let Adam Smith's "invisible hand" sway our socialist system, for that "hand" is motivated by bourgeois egoism. On the other hand, material interests in a socialist economy consist of not just those of the individuals but also those of other sectors. Only under state regulation can the interests of all sectors be properly integrated. The development of a socialist economy, therefore, calls for both planning and the market. For instance, a consumer's choice based on his preference, or production based on a single enterprise's decision, may or may not coincide with the overall social interest. If those decisions were made by the market forces alone, they might not result in an optimal and rational allocation of manpower, funds, and resources. Nor would they necessarily conform to the requirements of social development.

In the course of rapid socialist industrialization and modernization, the industrial structure and the productive forces are often subject to sudden, sharp changes. If every decision is made by the market mechanism, the productive forces and the industrial structure could not adjust promptly. In developing a socialist economy, all such problems of strategic importance cannot be solved by the market mechanism alone but must be regulated by state and social planning. It is conceivable that an overreliance on the market rather than on state planning may distort the productive structure, particularly in remote, frontier, and backward areas.

Take another example: In a socialist economy, because of variations in material conditions (such as natural endowments, location, and equipment), income distributions may differ among regions. If not redressed by the state, this gap in income distribution would widen, thus defying the very principle of socialism.

In a broader sense, socialism opposes both egalitarianism and excessively skewed distribution of income. While opposing egalitarianism, we should tolerate some differentials in income during certain phases of economic development—to allow some people to be better off now so as to create the conditions that eventually will make all prosperous. Clearly, the regulation of income, which may sometimes narrow the gap and other times widen the gap, has to be carried out by economic planning and the market.

In short, to coordinate the activities of various departments and regions, to look after the interests of the whole economy, and to correctly handle the material interests of all sectors, it is necessary to intensify state planning while making good use of the market mechanism. Some people believe that economic planning and the market are complementary. Allegorically, one may compare decision making from a planned viewpoint as looking at things from a commanding vantage point and decision making from a market viewpoint as looking at things from the bottom of a deep ravine. Whereas the former may provide a macroscopic view but not much detail, the latter may present a microscopic view but not an overall picture. In a sense, this comparison is true, for state decisions are made in the interest of the whole economy and consumer and enterprise decisions are made in the interest of the individual. The principle of socialism is to take care of the interests of a whole society, including the state, the collectives, and the individuals. Hence, economic planning and the market must be integrated to harmonize those interests.

If so, can the national economy be strengthened by unified planning? The answer depends on what a planned economy is. In the past, people generally held the view that a genuine socialist planned economy is one in which high authorities set production targets. Thus, unified planning was equated with centralized leadership. The state directly controlled all enterprises, and the ministries and departments of the central government would make decisions for the enterprises and the local governments. Ostensibly, this policy is detrimental to economic development. At the Third Plenary Session of the Eleventh Central Committee, a resolution was adopted that criticized the overcentralization of the state in managing enterprises. The characteristics of a socialist economy consist not so much of centralizing all manpower and resources in the hands of the state but of coordinating all economic activities according to scientific forecasts. It would be wrong for people to look upon the existence or absence of a commanding state planning and a centralization of manpower and resources as the cornerstone of socialist management. That would be a misconception. Then how do we strengthen economic planning by providing guidelines?

Our view is that we should draft long-range programs, particularly five-year plans, that will set goals for major economic development, fix ratios between accumulation and consumption, and allocate funds for capital construction and key projects, as well as improve the people's standard of living. Targets in the five-year plans may be broken down into annual rates, so they can be adjusted and revised if necessary. The state should focus on formulating policies and implementing plans.

Next, the mandatory section of the plan, which the enterprises must fulfill, should be gradually reduced until all planned targets become merely guidelines for economic activities. The state plans should forecast the trends of economic development so that enterprises and local governments can coordinate their activities accordingly. In the light of the guidelines provided by the state and the market, every enterprise should draw its own plan. Here, it is clear that state planning plays a significant role, for if an enterprise had little idea of what the trend of the economy would be, it would have to draw its production plans according to the market situation alone. But state forecasts can provide the enterprise with accurate information of the market trend. The more scientifically the state plans are drawn and the more the plans conform to reality, the better the enterprise's policy will be and the greater the possibilities of fulfilling the planned targets. Conversely, if the plans were drawn by wishful thinking or by command from the top, they would still be taken seriously. Have not we had enough bitter lessons?

The reform, in fact, will enhance the work and the responsibilities of the state planning commissions. Now more than ever, they are requested to produce scientifically drawn plans that can provide reliable information, which enterprises can use to carry out their activities.

To improve efficiency and to enhance the prestige of state planning, an enterprise's plan must be drawn independently, unit by unit and level by level, and the vertical integration of plans should start from the bottom unit, not the other way around. Problems concerning production, marketing, and the allocation of funds and other resources should not be submitted to the state if they can be solved by the market forces or contract. This policy will not only spare the enterprise unnecessary interference, but also relieve the state of routine chores so the state can focus on vital issues concerning the entire economy.

To ensure coordination in developing social production and the fulfillment of planned targets, economic policies should be so formulated that they serve as a guide for all economic activities, including price, tax, credit, investment, income distribution, foreign trade, foreign exchange, etc. In pursuing these policies, the state should encourage those activities that are needed and restrict those that are redundant, and thus help enterprises fulfill the planned targets.

Take raw materials for example: To overcome the underdeveloped state of the fuel industry, the state should speed up its development by granting it tax rebates, price concessions, and favorable credit terms. Conversely, to cut back the production of certain overstocked machine tools, the state should scale down the amount of credit available, raise the interest, and increase the tax rate. Thus, by pursuing their own interests, the enterprises will pursue their activities along state lines.

When the reform is carried out, the state should strictly enforce law and order, enact business codes, and set up a monitoring system—particularly by state banks, which will be responsible for supervising and auditing the enterprises' economic activities. All of these factors are bound to stimulate the development of the national economy.

The relationship between economic planning and the market in a socialist economy is exceedingly complex, and the problems involved in many aspects of management cannot be resolved in one stroke. The reform has to go through a historical stage. At present, China should set a timetable that will establish when the proportions of the various sectors of the economy are to be adjusted. Meanwhile, China should initiate reforms of its economic system, restructure existing enterprises, and elevate performance. In the course of the adjustment and rectification, China must carry out all necessary changes and open up avenues for further reforms. Only by trudging through the course of adjustment and rectification can the country properly handle the relationship between economic planning and the market.

8
China's Utilization of Foreign Funds and Relevant Policies

Ji Chongwei

In the present economic adjustment and for its future development, China will pursue an open-door policy. In the early 1980s, the priorities of foreign investment will be given to the development of energy resources, transport and communications, medium- and small-sized projects that require a small investment but bring quick economic results, and technical renovations of existing enterprises.

The Chinese people are determined to build a modern, powerful socialist country. This is indeed an arduous and great undertaking. As has been shown by the experience acquired elsewhere in the world, the effective ways to speed up a country's economic development and bring about its modernization are to draw upon foreign funds and import foreign technology in a positive and prudent manner and to develop economic and technical cooperation with foreign countries. In this undertaking, we shall adhere to the principle of relying on our own efforts while seeking outside assistance as a supplementary means and thereby pursue an open-door policy, which includes actively developing economic and technical cooperation with other countries. This is a long-term strategy. China is a vast and populous country endowed with rich natural resources, and there is great potential for developing China's market. Politically stable and united, the country is now working for the realization of the four modernizations: agriculture, industry, national defense, and science and technology. There are great opportunities for foreign investors to participate in developing China's industries and trade. In the past two years, we have had to make some readjustments in our national economy, and long-term plans are yet

Originally entitled "Zhungguo Liyong Wai Zi He Youguan De Jingji Falü Wenti," this paper was presented at a symposium on world economy held in Hangzhou on March 23–28, 1981, and sponsored by the Chinese Academy of Social Sciences and the Stanford Research Institute International.

to be drawn. Although we have hardly any experience to fall back on and we have barely begun to use foreign funds, we have made a good start.

Five Ways to Utilize Foreign Funds

1. Foreign Loans. We have reached agreements with the governments of Japan and Belgium for loans. According to one agreement, the Japanese Overseas Economic Cooperation Funds shall finance six construction projects consisting of two ports, three railroads, and one power station. The amount of the loans will be determined each year by the two parties concerned in the light of the progress of the projects. The loan earmarked for the year 1979–1980 was 106,000 million yen (more than US$400 million) at an interest rate of 3 percent per year, with repayment of the loan to begin in the eleventh year and the loan to be paid off in the thirtieth year. The Japanese Export and Import Bank has offered a loan of about US$1,500 million for the exploration of energy resources, primarily coal mines and oilfields, at a 6.25 percent interest rate. The loan will be repaid in installments for fifteen years after each project has been put into operation. The Belgian government has offered an interest-free loan amounting to US$31.5 million to be repaid in thirty years. It will primarily be used to purchase power station equipment.

As our memberships in the International Monetary Fund and the World Bank have been restored, the IMF has recently granted us a Special Drawing Right credit line equivalent to US$450 million, and we are consulting with the World Bank on the first batch of loans, to be used mainly for the exploration of human resources, for agriculture, and for the construction of power stations, ports, and railroads.

The Bank of China has signed buyer's credit agreements totaling US$12,700 million with the United Kingdom, France, Italy, Canada, Sweden, Australia, the Federal Republic of Germany, Belgium, Norway, and Argentina. As the loans are earmarked for limited, specified purposes only, and as our national economy has been undergoing readjustment in the past two years, not many pieces of equipment have been imported, and much of the credit remains unused to date.

2. Joint Ventures. Since the promulgation in 1979 of the law governing joint ventures using Chinese and foreign funds, several hundred contracts, consultations, and negotiations have been made between foreign investors and the interested Chinese authorities, regions, or enterprises. It takes time for the two parties to have a better understanding of each other's position, particularly at a time when our national economy is undergoing readjustment and when the pertinent

rules and regulations have yet to be improved, and so far, only a few joint ventures have been concluded.

By the end of 1980, twenty joint venture enterprises had been approved, with a total investment amounting to more than US$210 million, of which more than US$170 million will come from foreign investments. The projects include thirteen industrial enterprises, three hotels, one catering company, two service trades, and one pig farm. The partners in the joint ventures are mainly Hong Kong compatriots, but there are also businessmen from Switzerland, France, the United States, and Japan.

In addition, over 300 cooperative enterprises have been approved. The projects draw upon foreign investments totaling about US$500 million, which are mainly supplied by Hong Kong and Macao compatriots. These enterprises are located in the Guangdong and Fujian areas.

3. Cooperation with Foreign Investors in Offshore Oil Exploration. Four contracts have been approved. Contracts were signed between the China Petroleum Company on the one side and Japanese and French oil companies on the other side for the joint prospecting and exploitation of oil in the Bohai Bay and the Beibu Gulf in the South China Sea. A project on joint prospecting and exploitation of oil in the Yinggehai Basin of the South China Sea is being discussed between the China Petroleum Company and U.S. oil companies, and we shall call for tenders on joint prospecting and exploitation of oil in other offshore areas in the coming year. The essential features of these contracts are that the risks are small and investments jointly made; when commercial production begins, apart from operational fees, a certain proportion of the output will be set aside for China, and the remainder will go to repaying both parties' investments plus interest and a certain profit for the foreign companies. We shall invite public tenders for different areas and use different forms of arrangements according to the different conditions of resources in the future.

4. Compensation Trade. China reached agreements in 1980 with foreign businessmen for over 350 medium and small compensation trade undertakings. The imported technical equipment totaled more than US$100 million. In addition, the technical equipment imported for three big items totaled more than US$87 million.

5. Leasing. The China International Trust and Investment Corporation and the Oriental Leasing Company of Japan are jointly running the China Oriental Leasing Company.

At present, more and more talks on economic and technical cooperation are being held between Chinese and foreign business people, including joint ventures, joint production, compensation trade, and leasing. In the field of joint ventures alone, there have been more than thirty countries and regions involved, totaling over 300 projects. As shown above, China has started utilizing foreign funds, but this is still in the initial stage. There are many other areas open to cooperation with foreign enterprises, and their success will depend upon further exploration and the summing-up of experiences by both parties.

The joint projects approved by China in the last year or so were mostly of medium or small size, and the joint ventures in operation have shown good results in production, technology, and management. For instance, Beijing Airline Catering, a joint venture between the Beijing branch of the Civil Aviation Administration of China and Hong Kong businessmen, which began operation last May, has utilized imported facilities and boosted its production by streamlining its labor organization, training workers, improving its management, diversifying its meals, and improving its service. Its volume of business and profits have risen greatly. The joint Sino-French Wine Corporation, a joint venture by Tianjin and the French Remy-Martin Corporation, has brought the quality of its wine up to international standards since being put under joint management by utilizing imported facilities and technical know-how and improving its production process. The wine has been sold abroad. Joint ventures under construction are also making headway. For instance, the Xinjiang Tianshan Woolen Textile Company, a joint venture of the Xinjiang Urumqi Woolen Textile Mill and two Japanese and Hong Kong companies, has completed the construction of its new factory and is now installing machinery and equipment. Trial production is scheduled to begin in April.

It should be noted that the results of the undertakings, though initial, are encouraging. As far as joint venture enterprises and other forms of economic cooperation are concerned, China still lacks experience. In addition, there is a difference in social systems, and the economic management system in China is undergoing reform. As a consequence, we may face a host of problems on our road toward advancement, but I am sure that through our joint efforts, the economic cooperation between China and foreign investors will blossom and bear fruit.

Principles and Policies

China will continue, in the present period of national economic readjustment as well as in future economic development, to pursue an open-door policy, draw upon foreign funds in a positive and prudent way, boost foreign trade, and develop economic and technical cooperation with all friendly countries. There are many ways to utilize foreign funds. We might accept loans, including medium- or long-term loans from foreign governments or international financial agencies, export credit, commercial credit from private banks, and the issue of corporate bonds in foreign countries. We might also develop economic or technical cooperation, including joint venture enterprises, joint management, joint exploitation, joint production, compensation trade, and leasing. While drawing upon foreign funds, we shall at the same time import appropriate advanced technology and scientific management.

The principles and policies concerning China's absorption of foreign funds may be summed up as follows.

1. *To pursue the principle of maintaining self-reliance while seeking foreign assistance as a supplementary means.* China is a socialist country with a population of 1 billion so we must rely mainly upon ourselves—primarily on our own industrial foundation, technical force, and domestic market—to achieve the goal of the four modernizations while seeking all favorable external assistance possible. Our construction funds come mainly from our domestic accumulation, and the amount of foreign funds to be drawn upon must be in line with our capabilities of absorption and repayment. Regarding the policy concerning technology, we shall, in accordance with our needs, import such advanced technologies as can be adapted for our use, assimilation, or absorption. We welcome all foreign friends who are willing to invest in China and to cooperate in the fields of technology or economy in an amicable way. They will have equal opportunities and equal treatment.

2. *To abide by the principle of equality and mutual benefit and ensure the rights and interests of both sides.* China has consistently adhered to the principle of equality and mutual benefit in its economic activities with foreign partners. In any agreement on economic or technical cooperation concluded with foreign partners, we will uphold our sovereignty and interests politically and economically. We will not accept any conditions of a political nature, nor any clause that encroaches or infringes on our rights and interests. As stipulated in the law of the People's Republic of China on joint ventures using Chinese and foreign investment, joint venture enterprises must observe in all their activities the laws, decrees, and relevant rules and regulations of the People's Republic of China. The said law also clearly stipulates that "the Chinese government protects, by the legislation in force, the resources invested by a foreign participant in a joint venture and the profits due him pursuant to the agreements, contracts, and articles of association authorized by the Chinese government as well as his other

lawful rights and interests." "The net profit which a foreign participant receives as his share after executing his obligations under the pertinent laws and agreements and contracts, the funds he receives at the time when the joint venture terminates or winds up its operation, and his other funds may be remitted abroad through the Bank of China in accordance with the foreign exchange regulations and in the currency or currencies specified in the contracts concerning the joint venture." "The wages, salaries, or other legitimate income earned by a foreign worker or staff member of a joint venture, after payment of the personal income tax under the tax laws of the People's Republic of China, may be remitted abroad through the Bank of China in accordance with the foreign exchange regulations." The principles and policies mentioned above apply not only to joint venture enterprises, but also to other forms of economic cooperation.

Some foreign investors are worried that their investments in China might be requisitioned or even confiscated in the future. Regarding this concern, China's state leaders have declared expressly on many occasions that foreign investments are not subject to confiscation or requisition. With a view to legally safeguarding the interests of the foreign investors, the Chinese government has concluded an agreement on investment insurance and guarantees with the government of the United States; now we are conducting talks with the government of the Federal Republic of Germany on the conclusion of an agreement for investment protection; and similar consultations are also taking place with Canada, Japan, Sweden, Switzerland, and France on agreements of this kind. We shall also hold consultations with a number of countries on agreements for offsetting or exempting taxation.

Other foreign investors are concerned about the inadequacy of China's economic laws and about the possibility of constant changes in Chinese policies. These worries are unnecessary. As regards the enactment of economic laws relevant to foreign investments, they are indeed inadequate at present, and people at home and abroad are looking forward to an early promulgation of relevant economic laws and regulations. The Chinese government is paying a great deal of attention to this matter.

In fact, some laws and regulations have been promulgated in the last year or so. They include the income tax law concerning joint ventures with Chinese and foreign investment, the personal income tax law, the detailed rules and regulations for the implementation of those two laws, provisional regulations on foreign exchange control, regulations on the registration of joint ventures using Chinese and foreign investment, regulations on labor management in joint ventures using Chinese and foreign investment, regulations on special economic zones in Guangdong Province, and interim regulations concerning the control of the resident offices of foreign enterprises. There are also other economic stipulations, such as the regulations on the implementation of the law on joint ventures using Chinese and foreign investment, that are under study or being drafted.

These laws and stipulations will embody the principle of equality and mutual benefit for both Chinese and foreign partners and help clarify some points on relevant policies for the foreign investors. Pending the promulgation of certain stipulations, both the Chinese side and the foreign side, however, may go ahead with their negotiations for a particular project on the basis of the principle of equality and mutual benefit, and in light of concrete conditions, and embody the stipulations in related contracts and articles of association. The contracts and articles of association thus achieved will go into force, subject to the approval of the Chinese government.

3. *To create favorable conditions for foreign investors.* Much work has been done by the Chinese government to provide favorable conditions for foreign investments. With a view to expediting the development of economic cooperation abroad and the absorption of foreign funds in Guangdong and Fujian provinces, the State Council has approved the establishment of special economic zones within the three cities of Shenzhen, Zhuhai, and Shantou in Guangdong Province and Xiamen in Fujian Province. In the special zones, foreign enterprises and individuals, overseas Chinese, compatriots in Hong Kong and Macao, and their companies and enterprises are encouraged to invest in or establish joint ventures with our side-items of industry, agriculture, commercial undertaking, tourism, housing, and service trades. The special zones are creating a better environment for investment by providing various public facilities such as roads, wharves, communications, water and power supplies, and land leveling. There are also preferential rates for customs duties, land rent, and income tax.

Take the Shenzhen Special Economic Zone for example: There, an area of ninety-eight square kilometers has been designated for planned construction, including an industrial district, a business district, a tourist district, and a residence district. Industrialists and businessmen from as many as thirty-three countries and regions have come in for talks about possible investments. Up to the beginning of 1981, 490 enterprises had been established.

To meet the needs of transport for the growing foreign economic activities and trade, we are extending the port facilities of Qinhuangdao and constructing a new port of Shijiusuo in Shandong Province. Measures have also been taken to raise the loading and unloading capacities of the ports of Shanghai, Tianjin, and Huangpu. In recent years, we have built and are building a large number of hydroelectric and thermal power stations to meet the power shortages in the country. There are now sixty-one hydroelectric or thermal power stations of large or medium size under construction.

As China has a vast expanse of area and has suffered from an inadequate investment in transport facilities, communications, energy supplies, and urban infrastructure construction in the past, it is therefore very difficult for some places to resolve all their problems in a short time. We will have to tackle them one after another on a priority basis, keeping in mind our needs and our ability to meet those needs.

To expedite the utilization of foreign funds and the cooperation of foreign investors with interested regions, sectors, or enterprises of China for short-term or long-term joint ventures or joint production, as well as consultant service, the State Council has set up the China International Trust and Investment Corporation to develop economic cooperation with foreign investors. By the same token, trust and investment corporations have also been set up in certain provinces and cities.

4. *To emphasize the economic results and guarantee repayment and equitable profits.* When we bring in funds from abroad, we stress consistently that we will "abide by contracts signed and promises made." We must not only be sure of repaying borrowed funds, but also see to it that equitable profits are meted out to investors. With this fact in view, we must not overreach ourselves and must pay attention to fully developing the economic results of the investments involved when utilizing loans, importing technology and equipment, and running joint venture enterprises. With our past lessons in mind, we are making it a rule that before we agree to a specific project, we must carefully examine the project, carry out the necessary feasibility study, and make an overall assessment. That is to say, we must take into account the availability of raw materials, energy sources, and transport and make arrangements for the marketing of the project's products, the organization of the required designing and construction personnel, the ancillary parts of equipment, personnel training, and managerial skills. All of these factors must be included in the state plan.

We must see to it that the conditions are ready for actual construction and production, so that a project can be completed and commissioned on schedule, and that the products will be competitive in both quality and cost and readily accessible to international markets. Within a specified period of time, every project must have good earnings capable of covering the repayment of the principal plus interest of the loans involved and of providing equitable profits.

Thus, our projects using foreign funds fall into two categories. The first includes large-scale projects that require protracted construction and have low earnings, such as port construction, railways, communications, power stations, farming, forestry, water conservancy, and educational facilities. As much as possible, projects in this category will be undertaken using long-term and low-interest or interest-free loans with the Chinese government's guarantee of repayment. Emphasis must also be put on their economic results. The other category includes smaller-scale projects that require a shorter construction period or projects of scale that require protracted construction yet yield good earnings or foreign exchange, such as oil prospecting and exploitation, coal mines, machinery and chemical plants, light industry, and the tourist industry. The absorption of foreign funds, no matter what their form may be, must be made on the basis of responsible borrowing and using earnings for repayment. This policy means that both repayment and payment of profits have to come from the earnings of the project. Part of the products of joint ventures must be for export, so that foreign exchange earnings can cover payments for imported materials, foreign investors' profits, and the salaries for foreign personnel, thus achieving a balance of payments in foreign exchange for the joint enterprise concerned.

Priorities in the Utilization of Foreign Funds

China is now in a period of national economic readjustment. In our economic activities with foreign countries and enterprises, we will pursue an energetic and prudent policy that will be beneficial to the readjustment of our national economy. Absorbing foreign funds, importing technology, and engaging in joint ventures must be done progressively in order to contribute to correcting the disproportions in our current national economy and to strengthening its weak links.

Right now, certain sectors of the national economy are weak links. Energy lags behind demand; communications and transport facilities are insufficient; farming, forestry, animal husbandry, and fishery are not adequately developed. Also in short supply are consumer goods and materials for construction and packaging, urban infrastructure, and public utilities (water, electricity, gas, telecommunications, and roads). China has a sizable foundation for its iron and steel, nonferrous metals, machine-building, and chemical industries, but many old enterprises need technical renovation and transformation. In the late 1970s, China imported a number of large-scale projects, i.e., iron and steel complexes and chemical plants, and launched too many projects at home so the nation's financial resources were overtaxed. As a consequence, we have had to defer or stop a number of projects.

In the early 1980s, the priorities for using foreign funds will be:

1. Exploration of energy sources of petroleum, coal, and electricity
2. Construction of railways, ports, telecommunications, building materials, and the infrastructure in urban and industrial zones
3. Small and medium-sized projects, which require small investments but bring quick economic results, to help expand exports and increase foreign exchange earnings, such as in the light, textile, chemical, metallurgical, machine-building, and electronics industries and tourism
4. Technical transformation of existing enterprises
5. Some ongoing projects that have been deferred or stopped owing to a lack of funds

Before 1985, we shall try to reduce the number of new projects. Our efforts shall be concentrated on economically reorganizing the more than 300,000 industrial enterprises along the lines of specialization and coordination, of which the better equipped ones will undergo technical transformation and equipment updating, with a view to fully raising their potential productive capacities. Quite a number of foreign friends visiting China maintain that China has a fairly good industrial foundation and that it is funds, technology, and modern managerial expertise that are lacking. For some enterprises, their present factory buildings, equipment, and personnel at their disposal mean that they only have to introduce advanced techniques and key equipment or improve their management for the quality of their products to soon go up and their productivity and output to be doubled. Their profits will rise quickly.

We hope the foreign entrepreneurs interested in investing in China will consider the above-mentioned enterprises in terms of joint venture, joint production, compensation trade, or equipment leasing. In 1982, the United Nations Industrial Development Organization will hold a conference in Beijing to promote investment in China. Prior to the conference, we shall prepare a list of proposed projects inviting foreign investment for the reference of prospective foreign investors. We also hope foreign economists and managerial and technological experts can advise us on questions of economic development, economic management, and technology. Great and promising prospects for cooperating with China exist for our foreign friends in these areas.

9
Development of China's Foreign Trade and Its Prospects

Zhang Peiji

The primary tasks facing the Chinese people at present and for a long time to come are an active expansion of its productive forces and a realization of socialist modernization in a systematic and planned way. Foreign trade is an essential component of the national economy, and one of its primary functions is to serve the purpose of socialist modernization.

Development of China's Foreign Trade

The basic policy of China's socialist modernization is self-reliance; i.e., the country will carry out its economic construction by relying primarily on its own endeavors, on the full use of its own natural resources, and on the already built economic foundation. Self-reliance, however, does not mean isolation or seclusion. Each country has its comparative advantages and disadvantages. Through international trade, countries foster their comparative advantages by exports and overcome their comparative disadvantages by imports. With the rapid rise in national products and advancement of international division of labor after World War II, trade between countries grew by leaps and bounds. Foreign trade has become indispensable to the expansion of a country's economy.

At present, China's economy is still backward and the levels of development of science and technology are relatively low. Under these conditions, it is imperative that China should actively promote its trade so as to acquire advanced technology and equipment, as well as the goods necessary for production and consumption. If and when

Originally entitled "Zhungguo Dui Wai Maoyi Fazhan Ji Qi Qianjing," this paper was delivered at a seminar held at the Chinese University of Hong Kong, October 1980. Zhang was a member of the Chinese economic delegation that visited Hong Kong.

these items are achieved, the economy is bound to grow at a faster rate, the productive forces will expand, and the domestic market will be enriched.

Foreign trade constitutes an important ingredient in China's foreign relations. Needing a peaceful environment to carry out socialist modernization, China is willing to extend friendly cooperation and trade relations to all countries throughout the world. Shortly after the founding of the People's Republic of China, the government proclaimed to the whole world, "The Chinese people wish to cooperate with all peoples of the world to promote international trade and co-prosperity." In trading with other countries, China firmly adheres to the basic principle of equality and mutual benefit and insists that countries respect each other's sovereignty and carry on trade according to each party's wishes and needs.

Since the founding of the republic, and the development of the economy, China's foreign trade has expanded rapidly, at a rate higher than that of its national product. The value of the two-way trade in 1979 was 86-fold over that in 1949, rising at an annual rate of 16 percent or 12.8 percent in constant prices. In the same period, industrial and agricultural output value in constant prices increased at an annual rate of 9 percent.

Like the national economy, foreign trade in China has had its ups and downs, and sharp changes occurred during two periods. The first took place in the late 1950s when foreign trade declined year after year from 1960 through 1962 because of the Great Leap Forward; the second decline took place during the ten-year, turbulent Cultural Revolution when the sabotage of Lin Biao and the Gang of Four and their ultraleft line impeded the country's foreign trade. Although the causes of the two setbacks differed in nature, their adverse effects on foreign trade were the same.

After the ouster of the Gang of Four, China resolutely repudiated their ultraleft line and eliminated that impediment to foreign trade. From 1977 to 1979, the value of China's two-way trade almost doubled, with an average annual growth rate of 17 percent in real terms.

Over the past thirty years, the composition of the commodities in foreign trade have undergone profound changes. In the old China, trade consisted primarily of imports of consumer goods and exports of agricultural as well as handicraft products. Since the founding of the new China, imports of the means of production or producer goods have been increasing faster than other imports. Except for a few years, imports of capital goods have accounted for approximately 80 percent of the total value of imports. Concerning exports, apart from agricultural and handicraft products, manufactured goods have expanded, particularly textiles and light industry products. China began to export petroleum in 1973, and concomitantly, it also exported heavy industry products. Compared with 1953, the relative shares in the composition of exports for 1979 were as follows: Agricultural and native products fell from 55.7 percent to 23.1 percent; textiles and light industrial products rose from 26.9 percent to 45 percent, and heavy industrial products rose from 17.4 percent to 31.9 percent.

Based on the principle of equality and mutual benefit, China's economic and trade relations with various countries and regions have grown immensely. Because of China's geographical proximity to and its close economic ties with Hong Kong and Macao, the supplies to these two markets are significant, accounting for one-quarter of China's total export value. Up to now, China has established trade relations with 174 countries and regions, of which over 70 have signed bilateral trade agreements with China. In addition, it has signed several trade pacts with the European Economic Community.

Despite the rapid growth of China's foreign trade, the total value is still comparatively low, lower not only than that of the industrial countries, but also than that of some developing countries. Up to 1979, the total value of China's exports accounted for only 0.8 percent of the world's exports. The total value of goods the state procured for export accounted for 4 to 5 percent of the country's total industrial and agricultural output value, a ratio far below that of other countries. It is obvious that this situation is not compatible with the requirements of socialist modernization, nor with the development of China's foreign relations. Energetic measures are now being taken by the ministries concerned to promote further growth of the country's foreign trade.

China's Foreign Trade During the Period of Readjustment of the National Economy

In early 1979, acting on a resolution adopted by the Third Plenary Session of the Eleventh Central Committee of the Communist Party of China, the State Council shifted the emphasis of the Party line to socialist modernization. In June 1979, the Second Session of the Fifth National People's Congress made the decision to readjust, restructure, consolidate, and improve the national economy in order to bring it step by step onto a course of sustained, balanced growth.

The readjustment of the national economy aims at correcting the serious imbalances in some sectors of the economy; at coordinating the relative rates of growth among agriculture, light industry, and heavy industry; and at establishing a balanced relationship between accumulation and consumption. During the period of economic readjustment, agriculture and light industry are to be speedily developed. The process calls for the setting up of an order of priorities to determine which projects are to be built and which to be suspended or scrapped and what investment should be increased and what decreased. Appropriations for agriculture and light industry should be increased, and those for heavy industry should be reduced; the construction industry, energy, transportation, and communications should receive high priority.

Meanwhile, still greater efforts are to be made in innovating the technology of the existing enterprises, so as to fully tap their potentials and to raise their productivity. Thus, it can be seen that the readjustment of the national economy, by proceeding from reality, is an important strategic decision in pushing the socialist modernization steadily forward and a necessary policy in assuring sound economic development.

Readjustment of the national economy and development of foreign trade are interrelated and interdependent. The development of production through readjustment will make possible the promotion of exports, and a steady growth in production means adequate supplies of farm produce and sidelines for export and more raw materials for textiles. It will also be viable to improve the quality of exports and the quantity of imports, which in turn will raise the capacity for imports of advanced technology and equipment as well as other commodities that China needs, thereby ensuring speedy growth and a strengthening of the economy.

Some people abroad seem to worry that the readjustment will affect China's foreign trade and slow down the modernization. Here I dare to state positively that China's determination to realize the goal of socialist modernization is unshakable. During the period of readjustment, instead of cutting back on trade, China will expand its exports and imports more than ever before. Of course, it will achieve the planned goal.

In the course of readjustment, some construction projects that are not urgently needed may be suspended or scaled down, and there may even be a slowdown in certain sectors of the economy. For example, in 1978, China imported so much equipment that it exceeded its capacity to absorb. It is therefore quite likely that imports of such equipment will be curtailed for the years to come. On the other hand, the pace of China's production and development in energy, construction, textiles, and other light industries, as well as in communications and transportation, will accelerate. Also increased will be imports of modern equipment necessary for technological innovation. Imports of raw materials for construction and necessary consumer goods will either maintain their current levels or even increase their levels. All in all, during the period of readjustment, China's foreign trade will certainly expand.

In fact, since the readjustment last year, foreign trade has witnessed further expansion, and imports and exports have both soared. For 1979, the total value of China's two-way trade was US$29,300 million, an increase of 42 percent, or 23 percent in real terms, over 1978. Exports reached US$13,660 million, 40 percent higher than in 1978. Exports that showed a substantial increase included pork, fresh eggs, native produce, animal by-products, textiles, and chemicals. The value of imports amounted to US$15,670 million, or 43.9 percent above 1978. With the exception of steel, aluminum, and iron ores, imports increased notably in complete-plant modern equipment, materials for agriculture, inputs for light industry, and consumer goods. In the first half of 1980, foreign trade continued to expand, and exports rose even faster than imports. The January-to-June total trade value reached US$16,560 million, a rise of 26.5 percent over the corresponding period last year. Of the six-month total, exports were US$8,340 million, a rise of 42.6 percent; and imports, US$8,220 million, or a rise of 13.5 percent.

The above statistics show the correctness of and the necessity for carrying out the readjustment policy of our national economy. It can well be expected that further economic readjustment will ensure a healthy growth of the economy and foreign trade.

Reform of China's Foreign Trade System

The reform of the economic management system, which includes foreign trade, started in 1979 and will continue until 1981. What further long-range steps will be taken is still under study, so I can only venture some personal views.

Over the last thirty years, the current foreign trade system has gradually evolved under specific historical conditions. One should admit that this system did serve its purpose under the then-prevailing historical background and did play a positive role in promoting foreign trade, but circumstances have changed. Foreign trade in China has expanded so fast that the existing system, policy, and the machinery to carry it out are unable to cope with the new situation. To foster further development of international trade and to arouse incentives of all related departments, the current system must undergo some reform, whenever and wherever necessary and feasible.

Over the past year, some reforms were initiated in the foreign trade system. Guangdong and Fujian provinces; the municipalities of Beijing, Shanghai, and Tianjin; and other coastal provinces and cities have begun trading with foreign countries. More and more commodities are being gradually turned over to local foreign trade departments, which are now allowed to engage in compensation trade and in processing semifinished products. Approved by state agencies, some departments have established joint production and joint ventures with foreign enterprises for exports and imports.

Although the reforms have promoted foreign trade, they have also created some problems, mostly in management. These problems were brought to our attention by our foreign friends. Transient chaos is practically inevitable in the process of reform, but the overall development is sound. Like bumps on a rough road, the chaos will soon be over. We can eventually overcome the problems when we strengthen our leadership, improve our work, and streamline our system. The overriding idea behind the reform is to get all provinces and municipalities and all departments and enterprises involved in foreign trade and delegate to them more power to make decisions in order to achieve better coordination between production and distribution and to speed up the rate of economic development.

China's socialist modernization calls for the launching of an energetic export drive. In a highly volatile international market, we face keen competition, and to win in such a market, our commodities must adapt to market changes; our enterprises must have access to up-to-date market information, know what to export, and then wholeheartedly promote the exports with all feasible means. Such a drive calls for the joint efforts of all parties concerned. All provinces and municipalities and departments must chip in, the Ministry of Foreign Trade and related production departments should maintain close coordination, and enterprises engaging in foreign trade should practice economic accounting and be responsible for their profits and losses, allocation of funds, production, and management. When these reforms are carried out, they will rekindle enterprise initiative, improve management, and enhance foreign trade. The enterprise must be able to turn out products, meet work standards, and win in international competition; it must have a professional and competent staff with adequate trade knowledge and linguistic proficiency. These reforms, however, must first of all be approved by the concerned state agencies.

Similarly, the reform calls for a strong and cohesive leadership to conduct foreign relations and foreign trade, to establish regulations and rules, to coordinate the activities of various departments, to supervise and evaluate the implementation of foreign trade policies, and to incorporate local initiatives with centralization; that is, to strengthen management on the basis of active, mass participation. At the same time, the Ministry of Foreign Trade must help the newly established enterprises master the trade in the shortest time feasible, learn foreign languages, and enhance workers' professional efficiency. These are the utmost urgent problems calling for immediate attention, and we are confident that these problems can be solved through practice.

Under state planning and government guidance, our economic policy at present is "to develop comparative advantages, encourage competition, and improve coordination." The same policy holds for international trade. Since China has a vast territory with rich natural resources and diverse economic conditions, it should let the provinces, autonomous regions, and municipalities fully exploit their comparative advantages in accordance with their specific conditions. Competitions between enterprises and departments within limits set by planned guidelines and government policy should be encouraged, so as to increase commodity varieties, to improve quality, to enhance management, and to suit market supply and demand conditions, thus breaking down monopolies.

Moreover, to maximize comparative advantages and minimize comparative disadvantages, the enterprises and departments should push for joint operations on a voluntary and mutual benefit basis, for vertical and horizontal integrations, and for coordinations between industry and trade, between seaports and inland areas, as well as between provinces. The state should loosen some control at the top and gradually shift the economic system from centralization to integration. All these actions are bound to boost foreign trade.

The reforms of China's foreign trade system will proceed along the following lines. First, the provinces and municipalities, as well as some important enterprises that possess the necessary conditions, should engage directly in foreign trade and should be treated as independent economic entities responsible for their own profits and losses. Beginning in 1981, more provinces and municipalities should engage in foreign trade. Second, national foreign trade corporations should concentrate on a few essential commodities and serve as agencies of the provincial and municipal foreign trade enterprises. And third, the Ministry of Foreign Trade is responsible for policy and supervising its implementation, acting as the government agency in negotiating with foreign governments on trade affairs, administering national trade policies and regulations, promoting international trade, and overseeing all foreign trade enterprises. We are confident that the reformation of the system will enhance efficiency and expand trade.

Prospects for China's Foreign Trade Development

In his report "On the Work of the Government," delivered in June 1979 at the Second Session of the Fifth National People's Congress, Premier Hua Guofeng pointed out, "Whether in the three years of economic readjustment or in the subsequent years to come, China shall take energetic steps to develop foreign trade, expand economic cooperation and technical exchange with foreign countries, and adopt appropriate means according to international practice to raise funds from external sources." This is China's international economic policy.

Experience of the last thirty years has demonstrated that the key to expanded foreign trade lies in boosting exports. Whenever exports rose rapidly, our foreign trade expanded too, because exports provide the means of imports. Exports determine imports. Only by augmenting exports can we earn foreign exchange to pay for imports of advanced technology and equipment. Consequently, the principle governing our trade can be briefly put as "Exports take precedence, but exports and imports are interrelated. We will import what we can pay by exports, and we will balance imports against exports." Ostensibly, trade balance here should be construed as global balance and not just as balance with an individual country in every year.

To promote exports, we should first pay attention to those commodities that are to be exported. For years, the problems facing us in export have been that few of our products could meet international standards in quality, style, and packaging; we lacked the means of transportation and communication facilities; and the existing system inhibits expansion of foreign trade. To cope with these problems, the State Council, in recent years, has adopted a series of effective measures to promote trade and has created favorable conditions.

First, the central government has formulated a free trade policy, and as a matter of fact, the current economic reform started first in foreign trade. This policy has aroused the consciousness of the local departments and authorities who are involved with foreign trade to the need for paying attention to their work. Second, as a result of better implementation of rural economic policies, there has been a marked rise in farm produce and sideline products for exports. Third, to promote production and expand exports, more than ten comprehensive production bases have been set up to turn out products for export, including farm produce. The quality of these products has improved, variety has multiplied, and their marketability has been greatly enhanced.

From a long-range viewpoint, the industry that China has built so far over the years has indeed laid a material and technological foundation for further development. With the reform of the existing management system, the rates of growth will be faster and the levels of technology higher, thus enhancing exports. This situation is particularly true in regard to labor-intensive and traditional arts and handicrafts. China's rich resources and abundant manpower are the assets that should be tapped. Moreover, China is also rich in mineral resources. Its reserves of coal and nonferrous metals are plentiful, and efforts are being made to exploit mineral ores for export. The prospects for China's foreign trade are bright. It is estimated that for the years to come, the rates of growth of foreign trade will be faster than for the gross national product; therefore, the share of exports in industrial and agricultural production will gradually rise.

The composition of China's imports will not undergo any substantial changes. It is estimated that capital goods and equipment will still predominate in China's imports and so will some metals and raw materials for the chemical industry as well as food grains. Nor are substantial changes expected in the composition of China's exports, and farm produce and native sundries and textiles will continue to be the major exports. Efforts, however, will be made to push exports of minerals and chemicals. Although petroleum still plays an important role, it is not likely to expand rapidly in the near future. An increment in coal exports is not only possible but probable. With the readjustment of the economy, the expansion of production, and the advances in technology, China will export more machinery and electric appliances than in previous years. And that is what we plan to do.

Some people abroad are worried that too much export of Chinese textiles and light industrial products might flood the international markets, and they believe that if this happened, it would adversely affect the exports and domestic markets of other developing countries. But such worries are groundless, for China has an enormous home market in which production falls short of domestic demand, particularly for textiles and light industrial products. China will not, therefore, push for export of these products without restraint. Moreover, China's policy is to carry out foreign trade according to the needs and capacities of both parties at the prevailing international prices. At present, the share of China's exports of textiles and light industrial products is such that its impact on the international market is insignificant. It must be pointed out, however, that only when China exports can it import. A country may have great import potential provided that it is able to export. This fact is simple and plain.

Apart from pursuing the traditional means of international trade, China has put into effect in recent years other measures to promote foreign trade including joint production, joint venture, compensation trade, and the processing of semifinished products. These measures are only a start. China will continue to explore new avenues to boost its trade with other countries.

10
The Chinese Economy in the Process of Great Transformation

Dong Furen

In the process of socialist modernization, the Chinese economy is undergoing a far-reaching and thoroughgoing transformation. Parallel with the transformation of the economy, economic theories, which guide Chinese economic activities, are also in the midst of a great transformation. The purpose of this paper is to deal with three essential aspects of the transformation.

I

The first aspect of the great transformation is a change in ownership of the means of production. China had basically completed the socialist transformation of the means of production as early as 1956. Both in cities and in the countryside, the sector of public ownership played a dominant role. Looking back, one perceives now that although the transformation was not beyond reproach—in fact, it was pushed too fast and too hastily—it was, in general, a success, for the setting up of public ownership immensely boosted socialist production forces. But just when the guard against complacency was relaxed by the thrill of the success, China erred on the problems of ownership transformation and formulated some false theories, which led to a series of mistaken actions and thereby inflicted grave damage on the production forces. In the ensuing years, the mistakes have recurred time and again.

One of the fundamental errors of the economic theories on the problem of ownership lies in that they refuted the facts that the ownership system must conform with the state of development of the production forces, that the transformation of ownership could be arbitrarily car-

At the invitation of the editor, Dong wrote this article in 1981 specifically for this book. Its Chinese title is "Da Zhuanbianzhung De Zhungguo Jingji."

ried out regardless of the state of economic development, and that a communistic ownership system could be established on the base of an exceedingly underdeveloped economy.

Prevailing in 1958 was a theory that preached that "the transformation of ownership of the means of production should be carried out while the people are still living in poverty." The essence of the theory is that taking advantage of the state of poverty, the rural collective economy should be promptly transformed to the people's commune, which was communistic in nature and large scale in production. Likewise, taking advantage of the poverty state of the people's commune, it should be transformed to public ownership, so that the whole society could be transformed to communism—"to each according to his needs." Last, when the rural collectives became prosperous and the income disparities of their members widened, the transformation would be difficult to carry out. It was under such a paradox that a drive was launched in the countryside to transform the collective ownership of the advanced productive cooperatives to large-scale people's communes and to transform the people's communes from collective ownership to ownership by the whole people.

In the process of "transforming the ownership while people are still in poverty," some rural collectives, afraid to share their properties with others, massively slaughtered hogs and poultry, felled orchards, and dissipated their accumulation. Because of the egalitarianism, many members of the collectives that had already been transformed to people's communes lost their enthusiasm for production, which was how the catastrophe was brought to the productive forces. Although the "leftist" theories and practices were soon halted, they were never thoroughly corrected until the smash of the Gang of Four. Before that, production in many rural areas was impeded whenever and wherever the theory that called for "transforming the ownership while the people are still in poverty" prevailed.

One of the reasons why the theory "to transform the ownership while the people are still in poverty" was so hard to rectify was the prevalence of another false theory that held that public ownership is always superior to other ownerships irrespective of the state of development of the productive forces. According to this theory, the more advanced the level of public ownership, the superior the social system. For instance, the ownership of the people's commune is unconditionally superior to the ownership of the production brigade, and the ownership of the production brigade is unconditionally superior to the ownership of the production team.

This false theory ignored the fact that the private sector of the economy in rural and urban areas had already been integrated into the predominant socialist sector of the economy. Rather, the theory fancied that the private sector of the economy, which was to breed capitalism every hour of a day, must be eliminated. Under the influence of this false theory, the peasant's private plot was abolished; household sideline production, prohibited; and individual handicraft and tailoring services and peddlers were entirely liquidated. By 1978, only 15,000 individual laborers survived; but in 1960, there had not been a single individual laborer in Beijing, where in 1978 there were about 259.

As a result of the false theory, the urban cooperatives' ownership was systematically trampled on. Some collectives were transformed to state enterprises, and the rest were reduced to no more than appendages of state ministries and departments. Profits of the cooperatives were put under the control of the state administration on different levels, and the so-called unified management of profits and losses, i.e., the original cooperatives, were deprived of their responsibility for profits and losses, which were now the state administration's responsibility. Profits earned by a cooperative were turned over to the ministry or department, and incurred losses were subsidized by the ministry or department. By the 1970s, there was virtually not a single enterprise of collective ownership that was responsible for its own profits and losses.

The aforementioned errors created grave problems for economic activities: Supplies of daily necessities fell behind demand, commodity circulation slowed down, services were hard to get, more and more enterprises ran in the red, unemployment rose, the people's livelihood was impoverished, and a number of traditional handicrafts and restaurants disappeared. In a short span of time, the urban commerce network dropped 80 percent, and employment in peddling, restaurants, and other service-oriented trades declined from 20 percent of the labor force during the First Five-Year Plan period to approximately 8 percent recently. Here, we can see how serious was the consequence.

Another gross error in the false theory of ownership lies in the fact that it called for uniformly setting up an ownership of the means of production according to the standard prevailing in the economically advanced regions, despite sharp disparities in the levels of economic development between regions—between the advanced and the backward, the center of development and the frontier, the prairies and the mountainous areas, between farming and livestock, the Han and the minorities. It is no exaggeration to say that since 1958, one of the primary factors that caused the grave economic setback was the mishandling of the transformation of ownership. In recent years, we have taken a series of measures to rectify the errors, and at present, the system of ownership of the means of production is undergoing sweeping changes, which are bound to have far-reaching effects on the economy.

We realize that in China, there are great differences in the levels of economic development between the primitive and the advanced, between regions and departments, as well as between trades and sectors. To accommodate the sharp differences in the levels of economic development, we should diversify the ownership of the means of production. We should not treat socialist public ownership indiscriminately and unconditionally as a system superior to any other systems of ownership, regardless of differences in the levels of economic development—as if, the more advanced the level of public ownership of the means of production, the greater would be the superiority of the system.

The fact is that any system of ownership that is compatible with a certain state of economic development and can promote growth of the production forces has its superiority and should be retained. Looking back now, we can see that we should not indiscriminately transform collective ownership of the means of production to socialist state ownership; nor is socialist state ownership necessarily a supreme and perfect system of ownership; nor was it necessary to transform the collective ownership of the production brigade to the people's commune.

Under certain circumstances, the sector of private ownership should be preserved and even developed within limits, for in many respects, its functions cannot be replaced by either the ownership of the whole people or by collective ownership. For instance, repair shops, services, petty trades, and handicrafts can be run better by individuals than by the collective. When run by individuals, these trades are more flexible and render better services. As supplements to the socialist state ownership, they create immense employment opportunities.

As long as socialist state ownership plays a dominant role in the economy, the existence and development of a sector of private ownership is not likely to breed capitalism. Hence, more recently, we have replaced the past policies of restricting, discriminating against, and even eliminating the sector of private ownership with a policy of active direction, proper promotion, and better control. As a result, the private sector in the cities has begun to revive and grow. In the countryside, private plots and household sidelines are not only legal but also encouraged, and in regions inhabited by minority nationals, in remote frontiers where people raise livestock, or in the economically backward areas, a liberal policy is being implemented to encourage communes to engage in household sidelines and tend their private plots. For example, to encourage peasants to raise privately owned livestock, the limits on the size of a herd that an individual household can privately raise have been lifted in some regions, and in other regions, slaughter and sales taxes on privately raised livestock are being rebated. The development of the private sector of the economy has played a significant role in enlivening economic activities in cities as well as in rural areas. To cite one example, for years, the sheep herd in Gansu remained below 10 million head, but it has now soared to 15 million because of the lifting of the limits on the number of sheep that a household can individually raise.

The enterprises under collective ownership have not only been restored to their original status but also have expanded rapidly. Many enterprises under collective ownership that were run by ministries and departments are now responsible for their own profits and losses. Instead of being owned and run by various ministries and departments, the enterprises under collective ownership are now owned and managed by the toiling masses. Thus, the material well-being of the producers is directly tied to the economic performance of the enterprise where they work.

Now the enterprise must pay close attention to the profits and losses, and the producers have a sense of duty and enthusiasm. The virtues of collective ownership (such as flexibility, adaptability, and efficiency) are being gradually restored, and a lively economy is emerging. In some localities, the development of the collective ownership sector has grown faster than that of the public sector.

While preserving the characteristics of collective ownership, the rural economy has also undergone notable changes. Some localities have set up a system in which compensation is based on the amount of goods produced. For instance, a production team contracts to raise livestock to fulfill a certain quota, which can be met under normal conditions. The production team will receive extra compensation if the quota is overfulfilled, less if it falls short of the quota. Other localities, where the rural collectives lack resources, may turn wasteland, hills, or swamps over to individuals for reclamation, thus raising both production and the people's income.

Most recently, a host of new arrangements have emerged as joint operations under collective ownership, for example, joint operations between state enterprises, between rural people's communes, between urban cooperatives, between a state enterprise and a rural collective, between a state enterprise and a people's commune, and between a people's commune and a production brigade. In addition, there are agriculture-industry-commerce joint operations, forestry-industry-commerce joint operations, and livestock-industry-commerce joint operations.

China has begun to jointly operate enterprises with foreign countries. Although these joint operations have appeared only recently, they will play an important role in promoting the country's economic development. The operation of state enterprises is also undergoing some changes, which will be dealt with presently in the section on reforming the economic system.

II

The second aspect of the great transformation is the reform of the management of the economic system. China's current economic system was modeled on that of the Soviet Union of the 1950s. Although the system does possess some good features, it also has a great many drawbacks. As early as 1956, when we were building such a system, we sensed some problems and made a number of reforms. However, because of our underestimation of the seriousness of the framework, no attempts were made to break away from the limits inherited with the system. Another important reason for the failure of the reforms was the fetter of the orthodox theories that boxed up people's minds, and the orthodox theories are not always correct. For years, people looked upon the Soviet economic model as the only valid model for building a socialist economy and thought there could be no deviation from it. Specifically, there were two salient points of theory that blunted our perception for a long time and blocked our view so that we could not see how the economy should operate.

One of the two points was our misconception of a socialist economy as a sort of natural economy in which production is managed in physical terms and commodities are construed as something exogenous, existing independently of the system. According to this view, commodity production and circulation, if preserved in the socialist economy, are not the final goal of socialism—which is public ownership by the whole people. The view holds that commodity production survives in a socialist economy because collective ownership still exists; therefore, the scope of commodity production and circulation should be restricted. Means of production should no longer be treated as commodities, and all economic activities are subject to state plans handed down from above; the price system is nothing but an instrument of calculation and is deprived of the functions of regulating supply and demand. Otherwise, this view contends, there would be no central planning, which could lead to a restoration of capitalism. It was on the concept of a natural economy that our economic theory was built and our socialist construction was guided.

The other point is that for a long time, we overlooked economic interest as an internal driving force for economic development. The enterprise especially was stripped of its independent economic interest; it has been reduced to an appendage of various ministries or departments and has no right to take its own economic interest into consideration when making decisions. All its economic activities, such as what to produce and how much, are determined by the higher-level state organs and are to be carried out according to administrative directives. An enterprise must turn its profits over to the state and receive subsidies if losses are incurred. Since the enterprise is not responsible for either its profits or its losses, the economic interest of the staff and workers has no direct relationship to the performance of the enterprise. Whether the enterprise's performance is efficient or not does not affect the income of the staff and workers.

The economic system built on such a theoretical foundation created many drawbacks, of which outstanding ones are the lack of flexibility, inefficiency, and waste. The economic system has turned into a stumbling block to our economic development and must be thoroughly overhauled. Right now, we are preparing the way for a revision of the whole system, and meanwhile, we are making selective reforms on a trial basis. Over 6,600 enterprises have undergone an experiment through which some obsolete theories and systems have been proved invalid.

Ostensibly, the view that asserts that there is only one correct model on which to build a socialist economy is wrong. As a new social order, socialism must be created through practice. Being a large socialist country possessing many unique social and historical traditions, China should search through practice for a socialist economic model that fits its conditions. The purpose of the current reform is to attempt to seek and create such a socialist economic model.

Although some details have yet to be ironed out in the final draft of the reform, the general direction is clear. Of the issues to be resolved, two are fundamental in my opinion. One is the machinery that regulates economic activities, and the other is the driving power for economic development.

As to the machinery that regulates economic activities, this refers to the market. The mechanism that was employed in the past to regulate economic activities, relying on administrative directives imposed from the top, is now to be replaced by the market under unified planning. In other words, economic activities in a socialist planned economy are to be regulated by virtue of the market.

This is a fundamental reform of our economic system. When the market is used to regulate economic activities under unified planning, then all economic relations become commodity in nature; i.e., the means of production are to be treated as commodities. Correspondingly, we must pay attention to making use of the economic leverages—including money, price, interest, credit, and profit—that are closely related to a commodity economy. The economic leverages should be employed in such a way that they can regulate economic activities in line with the planned direction and planned targets can be achieved.

With regard to the driving force of economic development, this refers to the problem of how to shift initiative and incentive from the state administration to the enterprise; i.e., given the overall social interest, how to motivate an enterprise by enhancing its economic interest so that it will take initiatives to improve management. To achieve this aim, the economic interests of the staff and workers must be directly tied to the performance of the enterprise. When the enterprise earns profits, it should be allowed to draw a portion of the profit to improve technology, expand production, or set up funds for welfare or bonuses. Thus, the enterprise, its staff and workers, would pay attention to performance and would be concerned about whether the products meet market demand or whether technological innovation is necessary, instead of mechanically fulfilling planned targets imposed from above without paying any attention to the enterprises performance and without worrying about whether or not the products are marketable or whether the enterprise is making or losing money. The current reform will make the regulation of economic activities more efficient and flexible and achieve better results.

Based on the aforementioned reforms, a number of profound changes will take place in our economic system. These changes will focus mainly on relationships. First, the relationship between the state and enterprises will shift from one of administration in which the higher levels impose orders on the lower levels to an economic one in which the state will guide and the enterprises will be guided; the state will coordinate, and the enterprises will be coordinated. The state will no longer rely simply on administrative directives to regulate and coordinate enterprise activities; instead, it will rely on economic leverages.

Discrepancies and inconsistencies are bound to crop up between the activities planned by the state based on an overall consideration of the national economy, on the one hand, and the activities arranged by the individual enterprises based on a consideration of their own economic interest and the market conditions, on the other hand. But such discrepancies and inconsistencies should be resolved by economic leverages rather than by administrative directives. However, when the state chooses economic leverages to guide and coordinate enterprise activities, there is no guarantee that nothing will run counter to objective economic laws. But since there is market regulation now and the economic mechanism is flexible, discrepancies and inconsistencies, even if they occur, can be easily and swiftly ironed out.

The second change concerns the relationship between enterprises. Instead of maintaining indirect contact through the state, enterprises should establish a direct commodity trade relationship through the market, which will overcome the irrational relationship administratively set up between regions and departments and the arbitrary division of labor. For example, currently, two adjacent districts are not allowed to trade commodities directly unless they belong to the same administration. Commodity trade must detour through the administration of one district to the administration of another district. Take another example. When two enterprises in the same locality belong to different departments, they are not allowed to have direct commodity trade relations, which can only be maintained through the respective departments that have jurisdiction over the concerned enterprises. Such relations can only be set up indirectly through their respective administrations. When commodity trade relations are directly set up between enterprises, they will overcome the disruption that occurred frequently in the past between production and marketing, and they will define rigorously the economic rights and the obligations of the enterprises.

The third aspect concerns the relationship between the enterprise and its staff and workers. When an employee's income is closely tied to the performance of the enterprise, not only will he actively engage in production and participate in management, but the enterprise itself will strive to enhance its performance, for now the enterprise is responsible for its own profits and losses.

To be sure, there will be difficulties along the course of reform. One of the greatest difficulties is how to integrate economic planning with market regulation; i.e., how to reconcile the economic interests of the enterprise and its employees, on the one hand, and those of the whole society, on the other. In other words, how can enterprise profits be accommodated to the overall goal of socialist economy; namely, to satisfy people's needs? These problems are to be resolved in practice.

The current experiments in economic reform are confined to the enterprise's right of making decisions and primarily to allowing it to retain a portion of its earned profits after having fulfilled the planned targets. In addition, it can retain 60 percent of the depreciation fund for innovation of technology and equipment, and it is allowed to market its products after the planned targets are fulfilled. Some means of production may also be traded on the market. Products not under state unified procurement may be traded freely, and their prices may fluctuate according to market supply and demand.

Although these are just some preliminary reforms, they have already achieved good results. The drawbacks in the system—such as inefficiency, inflexibility, and waste—have improved, and many enterprises that have participated in the experiments have turned losses into profits.

III

The third aspect of the transformation is the restructuring of the economy. The present economic structure of China has formed gradually during the thirty years since the founding of the republic, and it has some serious problems. First, it is a closed economy. Foreign trade accounts for only a fraction of the economy, and there is a low import and export capacity and a lack of ability to compete in the international market. All regions have more or less similar economic characteristics, namely, a closed economy, each seeking autarky.

Second, there are grave disproportions among the productive departments. For example, heavy industry grew so fast that it was out of pace with agriculture and light industry while, within heavy industry, development of the sector that is related to agriculture and light industry fell behind. In agriculture, stress was one-sidedly placed on developing crops at the expense of animal husbandry, fishery, and forestry, and in the crop sector, priority was accorded to grain at the expense of economic crops. The scale of capital construction was extended beyond the capacity of the national economy, the supplies of raw materials and energy fell behind the development of light industry, and transportation and communication services lagged behind the demand of all industries. Moreover, the development of culture, education, public hygiene, housing, and urban construction were all grossly neglected.

The formation of such an odd economic structure cannot be separated from the errors in the economic theories and policies. There are at least two factors that may account for the errors. First is the misinterpretation of self-reliance, which was construed as complete self-sufficiency. Since the founding of the republic, China has pursued a policy of self-reliance, i.e., relying primarily on its own efforts, but supplemented by foreign assistance, and this is a correct policy. Being a large socialist country, China can rely only on its own efforts to carry out economic construction. Not only should capital construction funds be accumulated from internal sources, but the materials and technology needed in economic development have to be provided by the country itself. For this purpose, we coined a catch phrase: to establish an independent economy and a comprehensive industrial structure.

Undoubtedly, this policy is necessary and correct, but it takes time to set up such a system. Moreover, foreign trade should be promoted, rather than restricted, during and after establishing such an economic system. Through the international division of labor, we can export those commodities for which we have a comparative advantage and import those commodities for which we have a comparative disadvantage. Similarly, we should conditionally make use of, rather than preclude, external funds, which can make up the deficiency in domestic fund. But in the past, we wrongly sought after complete self-sufficiency and even treated external economic relations from an out-of-date moral viewpoint. We looked upon imports of foreign goods and capital as something disgraceful. Ignoring the potential economic gains and our declining foreign credit, we produced useless products at high costs.

Affected by this view, regions, departments, and enterprises were soon caught up with the idea of complete self-sufficiency. Pursuing autarky, quite a few regions (provinces, autonomous regions, and even counties) disregarded their respective comparative advantages and disadvantages and set up their own comprehensive systems to reach out for self-sufficiency. Because so many enterprises set up comprehensive factories, production overlapped among regions and among departments, and capital construction became increasingly inflated. For instance, in order to achieve self-sufficiency, regions suitable for planting sugarcane, fruits, or other economic crops were forced to grow grain; regions that had a comparative advantage in producing exports were compelled to engage in other activities; some regions even attempted to set up factories without regard to the exorbitant costs or to shortages of raw materials and energy.

Next, the setbacks in the economic development could be attributable to the lopsided stress on heavy industry. Tempted by the cherished aspiration to achieve self-sufficiency, we rushed to build a heavy industrial foundation, upon which it was hoped we could turn out advanced technology as a substitute for imports and modern capital goods in equipping light industry and agriculture. We did not bother to analyze whether or not we had the ability and capacity to realize the goal. That haste resulted in grave consequences to the economy.

For example, the haste to develop capital-intensive heavy industry adversely affected accumulation and overextended the scope of capital construction. Tying up large amounts of capital for heavy industry handicapped the development of agriculture and light industry and also strained supplies of energy and consumer goods, as well as the services of transportation and communications.

That is not all. For years, we pursued a policy of "taking steel as the lead" and focused all economic activities on steel production. To fulfill the production targets, agriculture and light industry were often deprived of raw materials and energy. This one-sided stress on heavy industry, particularly on iron and steel, caused disproportionate growths of heavy industry on the one hand and agriculture and light industry on the other. During the period 1949 through 1978, the gross value product of heavy industry multiplied 90.6 times, but those of agriculture and light industry rose only 2.4-fold and 19.8-fold, respectively. Therein lies the crux of the problem of China's economic structure. All other problems can be more or less attributed to the same source.

In recent years, we have been in the midst of readjusting and reforming the old economic structure. That closed, self-sufficient economic structure is undergoing transformation, and foreign trade has received particular attention. We are taking all measures feasible to expand our economic relations with other countries, establishing special economic districts to attract foreign investment and searching for commodities that have export potential and are capable of competing in the international market. Meanwhile, we will enhance enterprise's productivity and capability, let individual districts tap their respective comparative advantages, overcome their respective disadvantages, gradually break away from complete autarky, and practice regional division of labor as well as interregional coordination. We are paying more and more attention to both international economic transactions and interregional economic transactions.

The one-sided emphasis on heavy industry, particularly iron and steel, is being corrected. In recent years, heavy industry has begun to reduce its speed, and that of light industry has accelerated. Compared to 1978, heavy industry rose 7.4 percent in 1979 and light industry, 9 percent. If compared to the same period last year, heavy industry grew 6.3 percent for the first half of 1980, and light industry grew 24.2 percent.

Within heavy industry, the structure is undergoing some readjustment and reform. Some departments that support agriculture and light industry are growing at a faster rate than before, and more attention is paid to developing agriculture. For instance, the procurement prices of eighteen major staples were raised last year, averaging 25 percent higher than the previous year, while the state has exempted agricultural taxes for those rural production brigades that have a low income and reduced industrial and commerce levies for enterprises run by people's communes.

With the slowdown of heavy industry and a retrenching in capital construction, the strain on energy, transportation, and communications has been relieved. Proportions of investment funds to be allocated are also under adjustment, and more funds are being allocated for developing agriculture, light industry, culture, education, public hygiene, science, housing, and urban construction.

We can predict that with the readjustment and the restructuring of the national economy, China will expand its economic relations all over the world. A new rational economic system, together with expanded world economic relations, will enable China's economy to grow faster than ever before.

Glossary

Accumulation. Karl Marx defined accumulation as "Employing surplus value as capital, reconverting it into capital, is called accumulation of capital" (Karl Marx, *Capital* [New York: Random House, Modern Library, 1906], p. 634).

Category of production. In Marx's analytical scheme, production is divided into two major categories according to the final uses of the products. Those used for productive purpose are called the first category, and those used for consumption purpose are known as the second category. The former consists of capital goods; the latter, consumer goods.

Commodity economy. The characteristics of a commodity economy are refined division of labor and large-scale production. Goods are produced for trade. Although private ownership of the means of production has been eliminated in China, collective ownership still exists. Therefore, according to the Chinese economists, commodity production and commodity trade should continue within limits.

Commune. To pool the resources in the countryside to engage in capital construction—particularly irrigation, flood control, roads, and other overhead social services—Chinese peasants were organized into communes in 1958. There are 26,578 communes in China. Some are large and some small, averaging 4,637 households. A commune is a joint social and administrative entity. Its functions include agricultural and industrial production, education, commerce, as well as security and defense (PRC, State Statistical Bureau, *Ten Great Years* [Beijing: Foreign Languages Press, 1960], pp. 43–44).

Economic accounting. An accounting and statistical device employed in China to evaluate the economic results of enterprises; a system analogous to managerial economics in a market economy. For details, see *Chinese Economic Studies*, ed. George C. Wang (forthcoming).

Economic laws. Like the classical economists, Karl Marx contended that economic laws operate independently of man's will. Unlike the orthodox economists, Marx contended that few economic laws are immune to change. With the continuous advance of technology, and thereby the productive forces, many economic laws would be subject to change.

Exchange at equal value. In a socialist economy, the value of a product is determined by the socially necessary labor embodied in it. So products that contain the same amount of socially necessary labor have equal value.

Heavy industry. Capital goods including steel, machinery, energy, power, basic chemistry, electronics, etc.

Law of value. Marx contended, "What determines the magnitude of the value of any article is the amount of labor socially necessary, or the labor-time socially necessary for its production" (Marx, *Capital*, p. 46).

Light industry. Consumer goods such as textiles, paper, sugar, confectionary, tobacco, processed food, and other daily necessities.

Means of production. Marx defined the means of production as "The instruments of labor, the raw material, and the auxiliary substances consumed in the course of production" (Marx, *Capital*, p. 620).

Mode of production. The way society organizes its production, distribution, circulation, and consumption at a certain historical stage, or according to Marxist terminology, the unity of the production relations and the production forces. For instance, the capitalist mode of production differs from the socialist mode of production.

National income (national product). The concept of national income is defined in the Chinese literature as that of material product, minus depreciation. The material product for any one year is composed of the net contributions (or value added) of agriculture, industry, construction, freight transportation, and that part of trade and communications that serves the materially productive activities (Yueh Wei, "The Method of Computing National Income," *Jingji yanjiu* [Economic research], No. 3 [Beijing, August 1956], pp. 48–66).

Overall balance. A planned general equilibrium of the national economy in which the manpower, resources, and funds available are allocated to the various economic sectors and enterprises.

Petty production (petty commodity production). Refers to the individual production of peasants and artisans who own their own simple tools and engage in small-scale production.

Price disparity. The price differences between agricultural and industrial products.

Productive forces. Defined in the Chinese literature as (1) the experienced and skilled labor force; (2) work tools, equipment, and productive facilities; and (3) the material objects. In a letter of December 28, 1846, to P. V. Annenkov, who had asked him for his opinion of Pierre-Joseph Proudhon's new book *The Philosophy of Poverty*, Marx wrote: "Their productive forces—which are the basis of all their history—for every productive force is an acquired force, the producer of former activity. The productive forces are therefore the result of practical human energy; but this energy is itself conditioned by the circumstances in which men find themselves, by the productive forces already acquired, by the social form which exists before they do, which they do not create, which is the product of the preceding generation" (Karl Marx, *The Marx-Engels Reader*, ed. Robert C. Tucker, 2d ed. [New York: W. W. Norton and Company, 1978], pp. 137–138).

Productive relations. In the preface to *A Contribution to the Critique of Political Economy*, Marx stated: "In the social production of their life, men enter into definite relations that are indispensable and independent of their will, relations of production which correspond to a definite stage of development of their material productive forces. The sum total of these relations of production constitutes the economic structure of society, the real foundation, on which rises a legal and political superstructure and to which correspond definite forms of social consciousness" (Karl Marx, Preface and Introduction to *A Contribution to the Critique of Political Economy* [Beijing: Foreign Languages Press, 1976], pp. 3–4).

"To each according to his needs." With the advent of communism, when the productive forces are so well developed that the distribution of the national product should be based on one's needs rather than on one's work (Karl Marx, *Critique of the Gotha Programme* [Beijing: Foreign Languages Press, 1972], pp. 12–18).

"To each according to his work." In China, the distribution of the national product is as follows: (1) depreciation; (2) net investment for enlarged reproduction; (3) building up inventories, including social reserves such as insurance; and (4) consumption, which is subdivided into (a) administrative expenditures, (b) social consumption, such as education, medical care, and other cultural activities, (c) pensions, and (d) personal consumption. The distribution of the national product, the Chinese economists maintained, should be based on work rather than on needs.

Unified procurement and marketing (planned purchase and supply). Since November 1953, food grains and edible vegetable oils have been placed under a scheme known as unified procurement and marketing, and cotton, cotton yarn, and cotton cloth were brought into it in September 1954. The state sets up an annual quota of purchase that has to be fulfilled before the producers are allowed to sell the remainder through the state commercial network (*Ren-min shou-ts'e, 1955* [People's handbook for 1955] [Tianjin: Ta Kung Pao, 1956], pp. 456–458). "Unified supply" means rationing in accordance with availability and order of priorities, based partly on consumers' needs, partly on the state's requirements for exports and commodity reserves, and partly on the classification of the working status of a worker—whether he engages in heavy or light labor. The quota, therefore, has been revised annually, but is subject to change at any time when the state finds itself unable to meet it. The rationing of edible oil has been chiefly confined to cities and industrial and mining areas, and cloth has been rationed nationwide from the beginning.

Selected Bibliography

CHINESE-LANGUAGE SOURCES

Newspapers

Guang-ming jih-bao [Guang-ming daily].
Interested in intellectual activities and cultural and educational subjects.

Jen-min jih-bao [People's daily].
Official newspaper of China, containing current government policy statements, economic reports, and statistical releases.

Ta kung bao [Impartial daily].
Hong Kong and North American edition; originally founded in Tianjin; the most influential independent newspaper in the country before the liberation; interested in economic subjects.

Wen-wei bao [Wen-wei daily].
Hong Kong edition; originally published in Shanghai, now in Hong Kong; editorials are pro-China.

Journals and Magazines

Jingji guanli [Economic management].
Monthly publication published by the Social Science Press, Chinese Academy of Social Sciences; interested mainly in management.

Jingji yanjiu [Economic research].
Monthly publication published by the Institute of Economics, Chinese Academy of Social Sciences; suspended during the Cultural Revolution and resumed since 1978; mostly deals with economic theories.

Xin-hua yueh-bao [New China monthly].
An official publication of China. Primarily a compendium of important government directives and selected articles on politics, economics, culture, and international relations; occasionally contains statistical releases.

Books

Chen Bojun. *Bashi niandai Zhungguo jingji* [China's economy in the 1980s]. Hong Kong: Xianggang Jingji Daobaoshe, 1980.

______. *Zhungguo duiwai maoyi ji jingying guanli* [China's foreign trade and its management]. Hong Kong: Xianggang Jingji Baodaoshe, 1978.

______. *Zhungguo duiwai maoyi xin dongxiang* [New trend of China's foreign trade]. Hong Kong: Xianggang Jingji Daobao, 1979.

He Xinhao, *Buchang maoyi* [Compensation trade]. Beijing: Zhungguo Caizheng Jingji Chubanshe, 1980.

Liu Guoguang Bian. *Guomin jingji guanli tizhi, gaige de ruogan lilun wenti* [Some theoretical problems on the economic management system of China]. Beijing: Zhungguo Shehui Kexue Chubanshe, 1980.

______. *Shehuizhuyi zai sengchan wenti* [On socialist reproduction]. Beijing: Shenghuo, Dushu, Sinzhi, Sanlian Shudian, 1979.

Shanghai Shehui Kexueyuan Jingji Yanjiusuo. *Shanghai jiefang qianhou wujia ziliao huibian* [Compendium of price indexes of Shanghai before and after liberation]. Shanghai: Renmin Chubanshe, 1958.

Xue Muqiao. *Shehuizhuyi jingji lilun wenti* [China's socialist economy]. Beijing: Renmin Chubanshe, 1978.

______. *Zhungguo shehuizhuyi jingji wenti yanjiu* [On some theoretical problems of the socialist economy]. Beijing: Renmin Chubanshe, 1979.

Xu Dixin. *Lun shehuizhuyi de shengchan, liutong yu fenpei du "Ziben lun" biji* [On socialist production, circulation, and distribution; commentary from *Reading Capital*]. Beijing: Renmin Chubanshe, 1979.

Yu Guangyuan. *Shi lun shehuizhuyi shengchan de C.V.M.* [The CVM of socialist production]. Beijing: Renmin Chubanshe, 1979.

Zhang Wenmin Zhang Zhuoyuan Wu Jinglian. *Jian guo yilai; Shehuizhuyi shangpin shengchan he jiazhi guilulun wenxuan* [Selected essays on socialist commodity production and the laws of value]. Shanghai: Renmin Chubanshe, 1979.

Zhungguo Shehui Kesueyuan Jingji Yanjiusuo Xueshu Weiyuanhui. *Jingji Yanjiusuo Jikan* [Collection of the Institute of Economic Research]. Shanghai: Zhungguo Shehui Kexue Chubanshe, 1979.

ENGLISH-LANGUAGE SOURCES

Newspapers

Los Angeles Times, Los Angeles, California

New York Times, New York

Wall Street Journal (Western edition), Hong Kong

Journals and Magazines

Beijing Review (Peking Review), Beijing

China Business Review, Washington, D.C.; published by the National Council for U.S.-China Trade

The China Quarterly, London

Chinese Economic Studies, ed. George C. Wang; quarterly publication published by M. E. Sharpe, New York

Books

Baum, Richard, ed. *China's Four Modernizations: The New Technological Revolution*. Boulder, Colo.: Westview Press, 1980.
Boarman, Patrick M., ed. *Trade with China: Assessments by Leading Businessmen and Scholars*. New York, Washington, and London: Praeger Publishers, 1974.
Chao, Kang. *Capital Formation in Mainland China, 1952–1965*. Berkeley, Los Angeles, and London: University of California Press, 1974.
Chen, Nai-ruenn. *Chinese Economic Statistics*. Chicago: Aldine, 1966.
Dernberger, Robert F. "China's Economic Future." In Allen S. Whiting and Robert F. Dernberger, *China's Future: Foreign Policy and Economic Development in the Post-Mao Era*. New York: McGraw-Hill Book Company, 1977.
Eckstein, Alexander. *China's Economic Revolution*. London: Cambridge University Press, 1977.
Eckstein, Alexander; Galenson, Walter; and Liu, Ta-chung, eds. *Economic Trends in Communist China*. Chicago: Aldine, 1968.
Gurley, John G. *China's Economy and the Maoist Strategy*. New York and London: Monthly Review Press, 1976.
Hardy, Randall W. *China's Oil Future: A Case of Modest Expectations*. Boulder, Colo.: Westview Press, 1978.
Imfeld, Al. *China as a Model of Development*. New York: Orbis Books, 1976.
Lange, Oskar. "On the Economic Theory of Socialism." In *On the Economic Theory of Socialism*, ed. Benjamin E. Lippincott. Minneapolis: University of Minnesota Press, 1938.
Lardy, Nicholas R., ed. *Chinese Economic Planning*. New York: M. E. Sharpe, 1977.
Li, Choh-ming. *Economic Development of Communist China: An Appraisal of the First Five Years of Industrialization*. Berkeley and Los Angeles: University of California Press, 1959.
Liu, Ta-chung, and Yeh, Kung-chia. *The Economy of the Chinese Mainland: National Income and Economic Development, 1933–59*. Santa Monica, Calif.: Rand Corporation, 1963.
Mah, Feng-hwa. *The Foreign Trade of Mainland China*. Chicago: Aldine, 1971.
Mao Zedong. *A Critique of Soviet Economics*. New York and London: Monthly Review Press, 1977.
Nove, Alec, and Nuti, D. M., eds. *Socialist Economics*. New York: Penguin Books, 1972.
Perkins, Dwight H., ed. *China's Modern Economy in Historical Perspective*. Stanford, Calif.: Stanford University Press, 1975.
Robinson, Joan. *Economic Management in China*. 3d ed. London: Anglo-Chinese Educational Institute, 1976.

______. *An Essay on Marxian Economics.* 2d ed. London: Macmillan, 1966.

U.S., Congress, Joint Economic Committee. *China: A Reassessment of the Economy.* Washington, D.C.: Government Printing Office, 1975.

______. *Chinese Economy Post-Mao.* Washington, D.C.: Government Printing Office, 1978.

______. *People's Republic of China: An Economic Assessment.* Washington, D.C.: Government Printing Office, 1972.

Wang, George C., ed. *Fundamentals of Political Economy.* New York: M. E. Sharpe, 1977.

______. *An Outline of Compilation Work for an Input-Output Table for the People's Republic of China, 1956.* New York: International Arts and Sciences Press, 1972.

Whitson, William W., ed. *Doing Business with China: American Trade Opportunities in the 1970s.* New York, Washington, and London: Praeger Publishers, 1974.

Wu, Yuan-li. *An Economic Survey of Communist China.* New York: Bookman Associates, 1956.

The Contributors

Xue Muqiao. Director of the Economic Research Institute, the State Planning Commission; Deputy Minister of the State Planning Commission; Director of the State Statistical Bureau; Director of the National Price Commission. Major works include *Socialist Transformation of the Chinese National Economy* (translated into English, Japanese, French and Russian) and *China's Socialist Economy.*

Xu Dixin. Vice President of the Chinese Academy of Social Sciences; Director of the Institute of Economics. Major works include *A Course in Contemporary Chinese Economics* and *On Socialist Production, Circulation, and Distribution.*

Dong Furen. Deputy Director of the Institute of Economics; member of the Chinese Academy of Social Sciences; Professor, Beijing University; doctoral candidate, Moscow National Institute of Economics, Soviet Union (1953–1957). Major works include *Dynamic Analysis of the Soviet National Income* and *On the Methodology for Determining the Ratio Between Accumulation and Consumption.*

He Jianzhang. Deputy Director of the Economic Research Institute; member of the State Planning Commission. Major works are "Commodity Production and Production Prices in the Socialist Economy" and "On the Policy of Economic Readjustment."

Liao Jili. Senior staff member of the State Planning Commission; Director of the Bureau of Comprehensive Planning, the State Planning Commission. Major works are "How to Improve the Nation's Planning Methods" and "The Chinese Road of Industrialization."

Liu Guoguang. Deputy Director of the Institute of Economics; Associate Editor of *Economic Research;* Professor, Beijing University; postgraduate, Moscow National Institute of Economics, Soviet Union (1955). Major works include *Some Problems on Comprehensive Equilibrium of the National Economy* and "The Relationship Between Planning and Market in the Socialist Economy: China's Experience."

Zhao Renwei. Senior Research Fellow, Institute of Economics, the Chinese Academy of Social Sciences. Major work is "The Relationship Between Planning and Market in the Socialist Economy: China's Experience," which he coauthored with Liu Guoguang.

Ji Chongwei. Senior staff member of the Commission for the Administration of Exports and Imports; Deputy Secretary-General of the Enterprise Management Association of China. Major works include "Economic Accounting and the Question of Achieving Optimal Economic Results in Enterprises" and "Industrial Specialization and Coordination."

Zhang Peiji. Deputy Director, concurrently Vice Chairman, the International Trade Research Institute, Ministry of Foreign Trade. Major work is "International Trade and Market Conditions."

Index

For Product Safety Concerns and Information please contact our EU representative GPSR@taylorandfrancis.com
Taylor & Francis Verlag GmbH, Kaufingerstraße 24, 80331 München, Germany

www.ingramcontent.com/pod-product-compliance
Ingram Content Group UK Ltd.
Pitfield, Milton Keynes, MK11 3LW, UK
UKHW022120190926
475702UK00013B/1562

* 9 7 8 0 3 6 7 1 6 9 0 5 3 *